Praise

'If you are looking to bring greater visibility to your business, brand or book, then podcast guesting is a targeted way of doing that. With her extensive experience as a podcast host and founder of Silk Studios, Lou has used her platform to make a positive impact and bring greater visibility to many women in business. In her book *Dare to Share*, she guides you through the whole process so that you can share your story and message across many podcasts, grow your community and bring value to a wider audience.'

> — **Parminder Vir OBE**, film producer and co-founder of Support4AfricaSMEs

'The growth in podcasting tells us all that this is a very busy place to be heard. Spotify state that this year in the UK alone, there will be 14.6 million podcast listeners. Like all "social" media, there will be those that shine and achieve the results and those that just make a noise. *Dare to Share* cares deeply about your success and also the experience for the listener – a critical friend in your life to help you use your time wisely in a very crowded market.'

> — **Penny Power OBE**, founder of Business is Personal and BIP 100

'Being a podcast guest can be such a wonderful experience and open so many doors for you and your business, but it can often be daunting. However, Lou with her expert knowledge, insight and coaching acumen talks through the process in bitesize chunks and ensures it's a very doable process that helps find the right podcasts for you and your business.'

— **Karen Campbell**, founder of Karen Campbell Marketing and Hotsy Totsy

'*Dare to Share* enables you to serve others with your story, bring visibility to your book or brand, and connect you to the wider community. It inspires you to live a life fully, courageously and most inspiringly. Why would you not?'

— **Dr Mandeep Rai**, journalist and author of *The Values Compass*

'In a world where podcasting has become a new art form, *Dare to Share* is the perfect guide for those wanting to bring their story to life via the airwaves. A handbook brimming with passion, poise and pitch perfect pointers, it's a must-read for anyone wanting to become a Michelangelo of the mic.'

— **Felix Henderson**, co-founder, Look After Group

'Lou uses her film documentary vision and dares you to share your story in this insightful guide to using your own voice in podcasting.'

— **Nicki Bannerman**, radio presenter and podcast host for BBC Radio Academy, The Influential Women Podcast and major brands

'Starting my own podcast just a year ago and achieving a top global ranking show was definitely due to strategy and showing up authentically. This book really drives home some of the critical success factors you need to have in place for your podcast to attract loyal subscribers, inspiring guests and invitations to appear on other shows. The guidance and practical tips given on sharing your story is perfect for anyone looking to grow their audience through this amazing media. A fabulous insight into what makes podcast guesting special!'

> — **Dawn McGruer FRSA FCIM** – best-selling author, speaker, strategist (host of Dawn of a New Era Podcast)

'If you are ready to step into your purpose and reach the masses with your message by guesting on podcasts, then this book is exactly the roadmap to get you there. Lou walks you through step-by-step how to determine your strengths, curate your story, bring power to your message and get you taking action. You have a dream and this book will teach you how to make it a reality by creating influence and connections using practical tips and tools for a greater impact.'

> — **Dr Tabatha Barber**, board-certified OB/GYN and host of The Functional Gynaecologist podcast

Connect with the world and
make a positive impact through
the power of podcast guesting

DARE TO
SHARE

LOU HAMILTON

R^ethink

First published in Great Britain in 2021 by Rethink Press
(www.rethinkpress.com)

Sol and Ruby, I love you to the moon and back
and I am honoured to be part of your life stories

Contents

Foreword   **1**

Introduction   **5**

    Who are you?   8

    Your guide   10

PART ONE What's Your Story?   **13**

1 Storytime   **13**

    Why podcasts?   17

    Scene setting   20

    Call to action   24

    The quest   29

    The battle   35

    The triumph   41

    Learnings   46

    Summary   47

2 Themes And Topics   **51**

    Passions   54

Learnings   58

Pain points   60

Learnings   65

Purpose   66

Learnings   70

Peaks   71

Learnings   75

Possibilities   76

Learnings   81

Summary   82

PART TWO Guesting On Podcasts   **85**

3 Pitch Perfect   **87**

What podcasters want   90

Learnings   94

Researching podcasts   96

Learnings   103

How to pitch   104

Learnings   109

Spreading your net   110

Learnings   113

Your worth   114

Learnings   118

Summary   119

4 Getting The Gig   **123**

Do the admin   126

Learnings		130
Listen to the show		131
The host		133
The listener		134
Learnings		136
Consider the questions		137
Learnings		141
Gift your listeners		143
Learnings		147
Technical rehearsal		148
Learnings		152
Summary		153
5	**Showtime**	**157**
Recording preparation		160
Learnings		164
Voice preparation		165
Learnings		169
Guiding light		169
Learnings		173
Getting in the flow		174
Learnings		178
Giving thanks		179
Learnings		183
Summary		184
6	**Spread Your Wings**	**187**
Shout out		190

Learnings   193

Engage on socials   194

Learnings   198

Episode airs   199

Learnings   204

Conclusion   **205**

Acknowledgements   **209**

Contributors   **211**

The Author   **215**

Foreword

As the host of Young and Profiting (YAP) Podcast, I understand the need for brands and businesses to show up across all media and social media.

I started my podcast journey three years ago. What began as a little idea to help others profit in life has – through consistency, creativity and dedication – grown to a platform with over three million downloads and frequently ranked as a #1 education podcast across all apps. In January 2021, I appeared on the cover of Podcast Magazine, and I also have grown my influence on LinkedIn to become arguably the most popular podcaster on that platform.

But I didn't do it alone. I had my first volunteer for YAP Podcast by episode #2 – my current business partner, Timothy Tan. By episode #8, just a few months into my journey, I had ten volunteers in a Slack Channel. They were fans of the show and had reached out wanting to help and learn any way they could. I had a lot of experience relevant to podcasting – I started my career in radio and had five years of corporate marketing experience – and I could do everything related to producing and marketing a podcast, but my team gave me the ability to scale while I was still working a full-time job at Disney Streaming Services.

As we got traction, many people who were in awe of what I had built so quickly – a #1 podcast, a super-engaged following – were always asking, 'Who does your marketing?' This eventually led me to launch YAP media, a social media and podcast marketing agency for top podcasters, authors, celebrities and CEOs. My volunteers transitioned into paid team leaders, and eventually I quit my corporate job at Disney. In just one year, we achieved massive growth: today we have 63 employees and a dozen high profile clients, including Kara Goldin of Hint Water, Brit Morin of Brit+CO, Brian Scuadamore of 1-800-GOT-JUNK and many other incredibly talented individuals.

Podcasting has been around since 2008. Its rise has been exponential over the last few years and shows no signs of slowing: according to Apple podcast statistics, the number of valid podcasts in March 2020 was one million and had risen to two million within a year. Podcasting has become a critical space for guests

– from authors, CEOs, influencers, scientists – to share their story, mission and message, increase their audience and grow their brand.

In an increasingly noisy world it is easy for business owners, entrepreneurs and creatives to be drowned out, so Lou's book is a timely, digestible and actionable way for them to increase their visibility by getting to grips with the power of their story, sharing it on relevant podcasts, bringing value to a new audience and creating a trail for listeners to follow them and become clients and customers. I have guested on many podcasts for this very reason, including Lou's own podcast, Brave New Girl. Podcast guesting is an invaluable part of our digital brand strategy at YAP Media and we encourage it for our clients too.

From Lou's podcast guesting agency, her podcast, her other books and her social issue documentaries, I know that she is passionate about giving a voice to those who are under-represented and those who are on a mission to make a positive difference in the world. *Dare to Share* is testament to her belief in story as a means for the world to connect and podcast guesting as an impactful platform to do so.

There are books on storytelling and books on podcasting, but I know of no other straightforward guide that brings together storytelling, brand-building and podcast guesting as meaningful and powerful forces for good in the inspirational way that Lou does in *Dare to*

Share. If you have a brand, book, campaign, message or mission, I urge you to have this book to hand as you set out to utilise podcast guesting as part of an ongoing strategy for growth, value-giving and impact.

Hala Taha, host of Young and Profiting podcast, and Founder of YAP Media
www.youngandprofiting.com
August 2021

Introduction

The power of your voice to positively impact lives across the globe cannot be underestimated. At no other time in the history of the world has it been possible to broadcast your values, thoughts, beliefs, skills, experiences and challenges in an intimate conversation had from your spare bedroom and see its effects ripple across the world. This is what podcasts allow us to do. With such an equitable and accessible platform at your disposal, how can you maximise the beneficial impact of sharing your knowledge, ideas and dreams?

This book will help you become a podcast guest with a nuanced story to tell – a story with epic themes covering topics that can be mission-matched with a wide variety of podcasts. Telling your life story or your business journey in this way will get your message out there, build your brand, sell your wares, expand your audience and make the world a better place.

Not only will you be bringing attention to whatever it is you're promoting – your book, service, product, expertise or campaign – you will be impacting the lives of others through the power of your voice. Podcasters need stories like yours to fill their airwaves.

There are upwards of two million podcasts[1] with listeners who are waiting to be inspired by your particular slant on life.

I believe that podcasting has the potential to be an art form, with creative content that captures people's interest and imagination. As with any art form – writing, filmmaking, music, art, poetry – there is a craft behind it: a structure to learn, a methodical practice, an artistry and a mastery. As a podcast guest, you can bring all of that to the mic – and I will show you how to do it.

Who are you?

You might be a business founder, an author, a creative, a campaigner, a charity leader, an idealist, an activist, an entrepreneur or an 'imagineer'. You have experienced the ups and downs of life, overcome challenges and adversity, learned lessons along the way, persevered, triumphed and now have a vision for the future.

Podcasters want to hear from you because you have a unique story to share. If you tell it with passion and pitch the right themes and topics to relevant shows in a way that they can't resist, you'll nail it. This book is for you if you want to increase the reach of your own

---

1   Daniel J Lewis, *Podcast Industry Insights*, www.podcastindustryinsights. com/apple-podcasts-statistics, accessed June 2021

podcast; have a story, brand, book, message, expertise or vision to share; or want to use your voice for good.

Before you can be a guest on your first podcast, you need to have clarity about what your story is. Think about where you can shine your light: who needs to hear you and where will you find them? Then you need to show that you come bearing gifts of leadership, compassion, courage and generosity of spirit that will enrich hearts, minds and souls. You will need to get over any fear and take up space on air.

I will help you determine which elements of your personal experience to draw on and how to tap into your expertise, refine your message and share your brand or story in a way that best serves your audience. They want to be intrigued, inspired, encouraged, enlightened and entertained, and you will learn how to do all of that.

All you need now is a journal and pen ready for note-taking, and an open mind. This book will help you understand and implement the whole process of becoming an interesting guest across multiple podcasts, telling a nuanced and varied story underscored by powerful themes and topics relevant to different shows. You will not only build your brand, audience, customers, clients, fans and followers, but also connect with a wider global community and make a difference in others' lives.

Your guide

I've written this book because I want to help you get your story out there. As a documentary filmmaker of twenty years, and more recently a podcast creator, I have spent many years drawing out people's stories. I know you need to cut out the bits that don't resonate and focus on what has the most impact. You will learn to do the same so that your story can be heard loud and clear.

I was once a shy, introverted, phone-phobic person. I understand the fear of standing up and being counted, of speaking out, voicing your truth, being vulnerable at the mic and telling your story under the scrutiny of your listeners. Knowing the courage it takes to be a guest on a podcast, I will guide you through the process of getting there as simply and painlessly as possible.

Let's do this together and dare to share, because your courage in stepping up to the mic will light up the airwaves.

PART 1

WHAT'S YOUR STORY?

ONE
Storytime

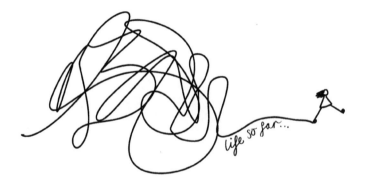

life so far...

I called this book *Dare to Share* because I have gathered that many of you know you should be on podcasts to promote your book, build your brand or get exposure for your campaign or charity, but you don't know if your story is worthy of being told. You don't know if you dare to share. You're not sure whether you have more than one spin on your story, to stretch it from one podcast to the next. You don't know how to approach podcasters to get on their show – and if you were to get on, you're not familiar with the tech, or the protocols, or the performance. And you're really not sure how to use the experience to create ongoing attention, traffic and sales.

Step by step, I will guide you through it all, so that you feel confident, ready to share and knowing exactly how to maximise each podcast experience and partnership. The first step is to look at your story. You are already the expert of your life. Maybe you have forgotten some of the twists and turns along the way. Perhaps the wins that seemed so exciting when they happened have faded with time. But as you work your way through the storytime structure, your memory will be jogged and all those nuggets and nuances will bubble to the surface for you to capture and bring back to the fore through the art of storytelling.

After working through the storytime chapter, you will have a flexible and adaptive story that reflects the life you have lived thus far, ready to share on a wide variety of podcasts. You'll have something new and relevant to bring to the mic each time, depending on the topic of the podcast and, no matter the skill of the host, you will be able to lift the interview with the confidence that comes from knowing you have a tale worth telling and lessons worth revealing. You will have a story with a structure that means the content can be flexible but will always satisfy the listener, because a good story arc is inherently engaging.

We'll be following five steps of the hero's journey:[2]

1. Scene setting: setting the stage for your story.

2. Call to action: the thing that got you going on your journey.

3. The quest: what were you searching for?

4. The battle: the big challenges you've faced.

5. The triumph: the wins and how to make sense of them.

---

2   A popular form of structure derived from Joseph Campbell's 'monomyth' in his book *The Hero with a Thousand Faces* (Pantheon Books, 1949) and adapted by Christopher Vogler in the twelve stage hero's journey in his book *The Writer's Journey* (Michael Wiese, 1992).

Your story will fit into a variation of this structure one way or another, as most stories throughout time have. We share a need to tell stories, to explore what it is to be human, which is why people want to listen. We have an urgent desire to tune into each other's journeys, with their highs, lows and lessons learned.

That's what we'll be doing throughout this storytime chapter, but for now let's talk about why podcasts are such a great medium for telling your story.

Why podcasts?

How you share your story determines how your message goes out into the world, a reflection of your life as you have chosen to define it. But why share your message via podcasts, specifically?

Podcasts, as a medium of communication, are growing fast. Perhaps in due course they will morph into a different form as new technology develops, but there is no getting back into the box that shaded us pre-internet and social media. Knowing what it is about our deeper selves that we want to project, share or draw from, will ensure that we harness the airwaves for the benefit of others and not for narcissistic exposure.

Our lives are clues to the roadmap of human existence. When we scratch away at our stories we uncover patterns of behaviour that guide us and others through the maze, negotiating work, life, love, loss, illness, divorce, disease and death. When you become familiar with the terrain of life, you will have insights to share and inspire.

For now, podcasts are the best place to set up your stool and tell your tale. Time will reveal the extent of their longevity. What won't change is humanity's need to exchange experiences, so you can take what you learn in this book and apply it to podcasts for now, and then to whatever new storytelling platform the future brings.

How podcasts work for you

The more we want to get out of using podcasts for communication, the more we need to understand, first about this emerging medium, and second, about what stories and lessons we can mine from our life experiences. Podcast hosts are committed to serving high-quality content to their listeners, so if you want to reach their audiences you have to first impress the gatekeepers.

You do that by pitching stories that have impact. You have the opportunity to disrupt the airwaves. If a host likes you and your story then they'll endorse you, giving you a platform to voice your ideas, expertise, pitfalls, inspirations, achievements and failures. It's all grist to their wheel. If they champion you, their audience will open their ears and their minds for you. If you have chosen your host well, this won't be just any old audience, but a targeted group of people primed to actively listen to what you have to say and who are the right market for your wares.

If you could afford a TV ad slot, you'd get thirty seconds to blow your trumpet. Unlike advertising, a podcast will give you anything from thirty minutes to an hour to communicate an in-depth perspective on your 'thing'. What's not to love about that kind of engagement?

Becoming a podcast guest is like being a roving story-teller of old; your role is to entertain and captivate your host and their audience with relevant anecdotes and splices of your life that capture their attention and engage them by sparking an enlightenment or reveal-ing a deep-rooted knowledge within them.

But how do you choose from the length and breadth of everything that has happened to you over the years? How do you find a thread that runs through the vast expanse of your experiences? How do you pick out the trinkets that will delight and empower others? What do you shine a light on for some people and keep in the shadows for others? Let's now get into the detail of how to construct your story in a way that will enable you to tell it on multiple podcasts without it growing stale.

Scene setting

So much has happened in your life, where do you begin? Don't worry. We're going to start by getting you comfortable with the idea that storytelling is something you already do, and that guesting on pod-casts is an extension of this that can be of value, both to you and to the people you want to join your tribe.

Guesting on a podcast is like sitting with a long lost friend and telling them about the life you've lived: the loves, losses, lessons and longings. You don't tell your friend every little detail; you edit as you go, knowing what's right for them to hear and what you'd like to keep to yourself. To another friend you might open up a different area of your life, with a different slant and anecdotes. When you guest on a podcast, you get to choose what you share in a similar way.

Maybe you think podcasts are something you 'should' do to help sell your book, build your brand or grow your audience, but what if they were also something where you could be of service to others? In this sec-tion, you'll learn why sharing your story on podcasts is such a great thing, both for you and for all the lis-teners who get to hear your story. Let's set the stage.

Standing out from the crowd

The problem is how to get your voice heard, with so much white noise in the world. Why should people listen to *you*? Whatever your wisdom, innovation, brand or expertise, unless it stands out from the crowd it will be lost. You need to be a splash of colour on a grey day, a foghorn in the mist.

Podcasts are a relatively new platform for sharing stories, but when you mission-match your narrative with what a podcast's listeners are there for, the stage is all yours. You'll be a podcast guest with an epic tale to tell and the courage to go deep with your story, to get it out into the world in the most powerful way.

I'm not suggesting you mine treasure from your tragedies in a pity-fest that will have us all staring gloomily into the soup of our own misfortunes. Nor do I recommend that you wave a cocky 'I've got this' flag from atop a mountain of money and success, because that's not relatable to most people. What I hope that you'll take from this book is a way to reflect the light off your lows, so that we hear both the gore and the glory of your journey, and in turn feel able to transform our own mess and mayhem into mission and meaning. In this way, we can marvel at the miraculous feat of humanity overcoming adversity. This is a way to help others, because in learning to tell your story and daring to share, you give listeners food for thought and show the possibilities beyond the pitfalls.

Your story speaks for you

Life is the tale we tell ourselves. Stuff happens, but it is how you shape that stuff into your story that determines how you learn, grow and feel about your life as you live it. You are the hero, it's your journey. You have goals and obstacles in your way, but you persevere, get your wins and your future evolves and unfolds. You have the burning urge to make something happen, and your mission will be your fuel.

This has been the common human story throughout all of time, across the whole world, from the caves to the Ancient Greeks and around the campfires of the Aborigines. From cinema to the family dinner table and the Friday night drink with your best mate.

Your story speaks for you. It tells of your truth, your tenacity, your reason for being. It is the wind in your sails. How you frame it, or choose to reframe it, reflects whether you feel miserable and bitter about what has happened to you, or have taken the blows and turned them into rocket fuel. Either way, in the telling and retelling, you shape your past, your present and your future. You offer yourself up as an alchemist of life, determiner of your destiny and an example for others to follow.

Stories trail through space and time like a spider-web constellation of stars. They are what tie humans together across nations, generations, gender, race and creed. Our stories are our call for connection and community. They are the call to the wild or to the homestead, to freedom or to the comfort of family and friends.

One way or another, we send out our metaphorical morse code. We invent more magical mechanisms to breach the void; from two cans and a piece of string, to the telephone, to smart phones, to who knows what in the future. Whether it's through chatting to friends, watching the news, reading books, watching movies or listening to podcasts, we're all responding to an essential need to communicate our stories to each other. We are bound by the tests and ordeals we must all endure and the triumphs we can achieve between birth and death.

People will love hearing your story and, each time you tell it, you will bring something new for every audience.

ACTION STEPS

In your journal, complete these sentences:

- I want to tell my story because...
- I believe podcasts are a good platform for me because...
- I want to be a stellar podcast guest because...
- My favourite podcast is... because...

Then, write a paragraph that sets the scene by giving your backstory, your childhood, early adulthood, culture and so on.

Call to action

This is the part of your story where you reflect on the moments that moved life forward for you, helped you to change direction or to escape from a life that was no longer serving you. When you know your life triggers, it makes your story more dynamic and you'll be confident that you have some gems to share with the show's listeners.

In this section of the book, you will gain an understanding of how to identify the big trigger points and emotional depths of your story and how yours can be made to fit into a simple story structure. We are going to focus on drawing out your story, but before we go deep, I want to warn you that this process can open old wounds and be somewhat of an emotional rollercoaster. As you jot down your story, remembering anecdotes and drawing out lessons from the challenges, you may find you come head to head with some deep-seated emotions. You may find this process triggering and suddenly be dealing with more than a simple canter through your life and work. Be gentle with yourself, protect the parts you don't want exposed, or areas where you feel particularly fragile or vulnerable. Your podcast host is not a therapist, so you are the judge of your boundaries and should pull back where it feels right for you.

Sharing is caring

Though you must set and respect your boundaries, the emotional landscape of your life is where things will get interesting for the listeners. They know when you are skimming along the surface and they won't feel as engaged as when you really let them in. You still get to choose what details you share, but if you decide to be brave in the face of the emotions that arise for you when you share your story and message, you will unlock the listener's capacity to engage intently with you.

As long as you feel in charge, open up as much as is right for you. This will give your voice authenticity. The listener will recognise something in themselves, be moved by your words, and you will have gained a fan and a follower. If you have acquainted yourself with the emotions that arise from memories or anecdotes, you won't collapse in a heap at the telling of them but will channel those feelings into something powerful for the listener.

Turning your journey into a story

Throughout the history of storytelling, we have learned to weave emotions into tales that speak to the human condition and shared experience of living in an unpredictable world. Storytelling is how we process and start to understand what we are feeling. But you can't just give voice to an emotional helter skelter by recounting your entire life story. You need some kind of structure.

According to Christopher Booker, there are seven basic plots.[3] There are critics of Booker's theory, but for our purposes his simplification is useful in creating a structure for your tale and navigating the emotional themes it touches upon. The theory goes that every story that has ever been told fits one of seven plots: overcoming the monster, rags to riches, the quest, voyage and return, comedy, tragedy, rebirth.

There are arguably a couple of other plots: a hero's rebellion against a greater power that finally surrenders, and a mystery, in which the protagonist, as an outsider to a terrible event, comes to discover the truth of what happened.

You want to begin your story by identifying your call to action. Look back at your life and think about the trigger points. Did you have an impoverished or otherwise challenging childhood that drove you to seek security through building wealth? Did you discover a love of ancient history early on that led you to become an Egyptologist? Were you inspired by your disability to start a charity to help others with theirs? I also call this call to action the 'anticipation stage'. It is the call to adventure, and the promise of what is

---

3 C Booker, *The Seven Basic Plots: Why We Tell Stories* (A&C Black, 2004) contains a Jung-influenced analysis of stories and their psychological meaning.

to come. Maybe you first felt this in childhood in difficult circumstances, or as a burgeoning adult finding your feet, running from the past or looking for something more than the lot you had been given. In a rag to riches story, for example, this is the stage where we find out about the wretchedness of your upbringing. This provides the backdrop to your story, painting a picture for the listener of how far you've travelled to get to where you are and what triggered the shift in direction.

EXAMPLE

One of my guests on the Brave New Girl (BNG) podcast was Tina Bernstein.[4] Listen to her story and then let's break it down into the narrative elements. Tina's story fits the **'overcoming the monster'** plot, telling us of the nervous breakdown she experienced in her mid-twenties at the height of a stellar career. She takes us deeper, following the story elements to give us a sense of time passing, drama unfolding and lessons being learned.

Scene setting: Tina tells of the shame that she inherited from a childhood of violence and abuse; of her father saying unkind things to her as a child, and how...

Call to action: ... she escaped from her family's clutches to attend boarding school in England. She was only a teenager, but she knew she had to get out of the home and managed to persuade her parents to allow her to go away to school. She buried the past and got on with

---

4   L Hamilton, 'Let's talk about anxiety with Tina Bernstein', Brave New Girl (2019), https://podcasts.apple.com/in/podcast/lets-talk-about-anxiety-with-tina-bernstein/id1462548683?i=1000456742790

school life, discovered she was good at art and was accepted to art school.

In the next section, we will look at the quest element of Tina's story. For now, it's time to identify your own call to action. It doesn't have to have occurred early, and you can have had many calls to action throughout your life. One of mine happened when I was fifty when my kids were flying the nest, my grandmother died and I thought, 'Uh oh, what now?' I picked up a pencil and out popped *Brave New Girl*. In that moment, my life changed.

ACTION STEPS

- Jot down in your journal any areas or events that you definitely do not want to share on a podcast, perhaps because it involves other people whose privacy you want to protect (for example, a divorce).
- Add to your scene setting if you've remembered more about your background, childhood, hobbies and journey to adulthood.
- Identify your call to action. What was the trigger for a change in direction? A defining moment? What have you run from, or towards?
- Add your call to action to your scene-setting paragraph.
- Listen to the interview with Tina Bernstein to acquaint yourself with her story.

The quest

Do you feel like you are at the bottom of a mountain? The beginning of any journey can feel this way. Remember, though you are learning how to bundle your life story into manageable and interesting chunks with direction and purpose, you're not writing a novel. You don't need to make anything up. Your life has happened, one way or another. Your job is to steadily work your way through the stages set out in this book that will spark your transformation into a stellar podcast guest. The great thing is that you are looking back at your life with the benefit of hindsight; you can see the roadmap you've followed thus far, with all its bumps, twists, turns and treats along the way.

In the last section, you worked out the trigger points and emotional cues that added up to your call to action. Now you need to work out what your quest was: to become a doctor, learn a language, change the world, live a different life from what you were born into, get a job, move countries…

In the quest stage of your life story, you challenged yourself, increased your knowledge, got inspired to move towards your goals. There are typically five elements to a quest:[5] the quester (you), a destination, the

---

5   Mark Flanagan, 'The definition of quest in literature', ThoughtCo (27 August 2020), www.thoughtco.com/definition-of-quest-851677, accessed June 2021.

justification, the challenges and trials along the way, and then the discovery of the real destination. Let's look at these different elements in turn.

The quester

Who were you at the beginning of your journey, once you'd felt your call to action? You, the hero, likely experienced some initial success and everything seemed to be going well, perhaps you felt a youth-like sense of invincibility. You went out into the world, discovering yourself as a separate entity from your family unit, whatever that looked like. Or maybe, like me, you embarked on a new quest, later on in life. Maybe at this point you discovered your passions, feeling like you had found your path, or at least got some kind of a handle on adulthood or midulthood. Think about who you were when you embarked on a new phase or adventure.

The imagined destination

Did you decide to buy a flat, move to another part of the country or take up a post abroad? Maybe it was more a feeling of being on the road to the life you wanted. Maybe it was where you thought you wanted to be: the bright city lights, an office in a glass skyscraper, or a veterinary practice in the countryside. Here are some of the destinations my podcast guests found themselves in early in their quest:

- Tina was travelling around Europe in a super-glamorous job.

- Emma was in a part-time job, living in a small flat, in a relationship with a young baby.

- Sharon was at art school doing an MA, discovering herself through her work.

- Nik was working in recruitment in the city, earning a good living.

- Liz was gathering momentum as an academic Egyptologist at Oxford University.

- Sarah was at the Southbank Centre, building a burgeoning career in arts production.

Where were you going at the beginning of your quest?

The justification

You thought your life was heading in a certain direction with some sense of your goals. You made choices with the knowledge and experience you had at the time. You thought you knew where you were going, and why you were doing what you were doing. For example:

- Tina wanted to live an independent and exciting life.

- Emma wanted another baby to complete her family.

- Sharon wanted to become a professional artist.

- Nik wanted a successful career.

- Liz wanted to study Egyptian graffiti and uncover the many mysteries of ancient scripts, society and structures.

- Sarah wanted to be involved in exciting arts projects, making them happen and supporting artists to fulfil their vision.

What did you believe you were setting out to do, and why?

The challenges and trials

Of course, even when you think you have a plan, life has a habit of tripping you up, putting obstacles in your path and challenging your status quo. When you look back, you will see the rocks in your path, the reasons you questioned and re-evaluated what you were doing. My podcast guests have revealed a wide variety of challenges:

- Tina started to get anxiety attacks every time she flew on a plane, which her job necessitated.

- Emma went through gruelling IVF, eventually getting pregnant, only to discover she was expecting triplets.

- Sharon had a tutor at art college who tried to undermine the direction her art was taking.

- Nik became increasingly unhappy working in recruitment and also went through a divorce.

- Liz contracted sepsis, nearly died and suffered life-changing disabilities.

- Sarah was made redundant from her job.

What were the challenges and trials you faced in your quest?

The real destination

There is nothing like an unexpected life challenge to make you reassess all your decisions thus far. This stage of your story was when you started to dig deeper into why you were doing what you were doing, where your life was truly heading, who you were, what you were about. You didn't necessarily want to know the answers. Maybe you tried to stay on the same path but the rocks flying at you just got bigger and bigger until you finally stopped and looked a different way.

- Tina had a nervous breakdown, left her career and started on the road to self-discovery and self-help.

- Emma gave birth to triplets, but then received a cancer diagnosis before also realising she needed to escape her toxic relationship.

- Sharon recognised that she needed to commit to taking up space and fully represent herself in the world through her art.

- Nik realised she couldn't work in recruitment anymore. She took a floristry course and realised that she needed to become a florist.

- Liz knew that she wanted to keep working as an Egyptologist, but that her approach would have to be different.

- Sarah decided that in fact she wanted to be a professional photographer and make her vision a reality.

What did you realise was your real purpose the world?

EXAMPLE

One of my guests, Ali Criado-Perez, was a trained nurse but had spent twenty-odd years travelling the world for her husband's job. Then her husband announced the marriage was over. Ali was devastated but picked herself up and did a retraining nursing course. One day she heard about the organisation *Médecins Sans Frontières* (Doctors Without Borders), thought it sounded interesting and applied, without much hope of being accepted. She was offered a job and sent on a mission to work as a nurse in a war-torn corner of the world. She never looked back.[6]

- The quester: Ali had stopped practising nursing and instead followed her husband's career.

---

6   L Hamilton, 'Nursing on the front line with Alison Criado Perez', Brave New Girl (2021), https://podcasts.apple.com/in/podcast/nursing-on-the-frontline-with-alison-criado-perez/id1462548683?i=1000473248547

- The imagined destination: travelling the world.
- The justification: it was an exciting and glamorous life.
- The challenges and trials: her husband wanted a divorce.
- The real destination: to use her nursing skills for the greater good by travelling the world with an NGO.

ACTION STEPS

- Who were you at the beginning of your quest?
- Where did you think you were going?
- What were your stated reasons for heading in this direction?
- What challenges and trials made you stop and reassess?
- What was the real direction you were meant to be taking, and why?

Now you have the five elements of your quest written out, you can start to see how your life story reveals itself with all its twists and turns.

The battle

The beauty of guesting on multiple podcasts is that all your battle scars will be interesting to someone, you just choose which are appropriate for each podcast. The biggest battles are often where the biggest learnings and growth can be found. This section of your story is about where you had to do battle, either with the outside world or with your own mind, so put on your suit of armour and let's dive in.

The build-up

You're on your quest, climbing that mountain. Let's say you've decided that on the side of your job you're going to become a writer and illustrator and in your spare time will create a children's picture book. You're excited. You knock up a vision board and draw pictures of yourself receiving the Best Children's Book of the Year award. All you have to do is write the book and the vision board will be reality.

Frustration

The frustration sets in when your vision of your future or dream outcome doesn't reflect the reality of getting the work done to reach it. In our children's book scenario, you show up for sure. Mostly. Sometimes you go and meet friends, scroll through Instagram or wash the kitchen floor. But that's not how children's books get created. When you do show up, you have a great idea, but perhaps it doesn't come out right. You screw up the pieces of paper and hurl them across the room.

Nightmare

The nightmare stage is where things get way worse before they get any better. You are actually making progress with your children's book: the drawings are nice, the words string together pretty well, and you feel confident enough to chat to a friend of a friend who used to work for a literary agent and has offered to give you some advice. A bit of feedback can only make it better, you tell yourself.

The friend of a friend makes some positive sounds, then comes the bombshell: 'It's nice, but you know nowadays they want it all drawn on the computer, so you, or they can make any changes they want. It's so much easier.' So much easier? You're going to have to learn a whole new computer program and start the drawings again. Nightmare.

The battle itself

The battle is the point at which you go all in, with no idea whether you will win or lose. It might be cancer, or a new business venture, or a relationship landslide. Whatever it was that you battled, it marked the end of one stage of your life as you knew it. At the time, you didn't know if you would come out of it alive, sane or whole.

Let's see where you've got to in our children's book scenario. Your day job is suffering from the stress you feel trying to juggle two priorities. Your boss is a nightmare and you're burning the midnight oil on the book. An opportunity comes up to take redundancy. The gods have moved to your side of the battlefield. You take the payout and finish the book. The battle is over.

The aftermath

When battles come to an end, there are after effects, waves of fallout. This is the aftermath. Returning to our scenario, you've jacked in your job and now you're a full-time writer. You've finished your book and are sending it off to agents. You receive many rejection letters; your hard won creation sinks to the bottom of many a slush pile. The bills don't stop just because you're following your dream.

But you know you're living the life that's right for you. You get yourself a part-time job, cut out unnecessary expenditure and live simply. Somewhere out there is an agent waiting for what you have to offer. You feel it in your bones and you stick it out.

The lesson

In all the experience of battling through the hard times, getting to the other side and dealing with the aftermath, perhaps even when you felt like you had lost the battle in some way, there are lessons to be learned. For your podcast listeners, this is the meaty bit of your story. What was your takeaway? What gave you the wind under your wings to carry on?

In our fictional story where you are a children's book writer, you learned that you were living a life that didn't give you enough room for creativity. You learned that if you took a leap into the unknown you could survive and thrive. You learned that even though it wasn't plain sailing once the battle was over, you could keep taking action, making changes, adjusting and streamlining until you were able to live the life of a writer.

The lessons were hard-learned but, looking back, you see that that is where the growth was. Daring to share these moments, revealing your battle scars, will have podcast listeners hanging onto your words and, hopefully, daring to make difficult decisions and take action in their own lives.

EXAMPLE

One of my guests, Dr Elizabeth Frood, an Egyptologist, was on a quest to build her career at Oxford University.[7]

Build-up stage: She had landed the job of Associate Professor when...

Frustration stage: ...she fell ill with what she thought was a stomach bug.

Nightmare stage: She became increasingly unwell over a few days until she was admitted to hospital with sepsis.

The battle: She fought for her life and lost her legs, the hearing in her right ear and much of the use of her hands.

---

7   L Hamilton, 'Surviving sepsis: Understanding courage after crisis', Brave New Girl (2021), https://podcasts.apple.com/in/podcast/surviving-sepsis-understanding-courage-after-crisis/id1462548683?i=1000489244745

Aftermath: She won the battle of life and death, but the effects of sepsis were life-changing. She had to adjust to living with her disability, to find out how she could be a mum, a partner and an Egyptologist with her new limitations.

The lessons: She had survived and learned that she could also thrive. She kept her job at the university, she went back to work on site in Egypt, her relationship with her son was unaffected by her disability, her partner was fully supportive, and she found she could also work successfully as a broadcaster.

As you have been fighting the battles of your life story, I wonder what lessons you have learned along the way?

ACTION STEPS

It's likely that you have had a few battles in life. Try this exercise to remember and structure the main one that springs to mind:

- What were you bubbling along doing, when you thought everything was OK, but...
- You started to get frustrated by something, or events took a turn you weren't expecting. What was it?
- How did things get nightmarish?
- Then you were in full battle mode; what did the aftermath look like?
- Once the battle was over, what were the lessons you learned?

Once you've identified your main battle, you can make quick notes on others whenever you remember them.

This will provide an arsenal of stories you can tell on multiple podcasts.

The triumph

Going on podcasts and sharing your wins shows that all the trials and tribulations were worth it for the triumphs. You may not have won an Oscar (or maybe you have), but every time you rose up after being knocked back, that was a win. Every lesson learned is a win. Every bit of recognition, every trophy, medal, pay rise, sale, is evidence that what you are doing is of value. Listeners want to hear about your wins, it helps them to recognise their own.

Resolution

All stories need some kind of resolution. When building this part of your story, we are looking for big triumphs to share or little wins along the way that showed you were heading in the right direction. A listener doesn't need to know about the structure of a storyline, we all have it in our DNA. They will have had stories read to them, watched films and read books since they were tiny. They expect to move from one part of the story to the next and they want a resolution, whether that comes in the form of a triumph or a tragedy.

Whether or not you feel comfortable sharing your wins, you need to see them as part and parcel of your story. They may be peppered throughout your journey, or the resolution may come in the form of one big triumph after a long battle, like overcoming cancer, taking your business online in a pandemic, or finally getting your book published after years of struggling to write the darned thing. Whatever the shape or size of your triumphs, podcast listeners want to hear about them, so decide what it is that you dare to share.

Bittersweet

Sometimes a triumph comes in the form of a bitter pill, an experience that, at the time, felt like your life was going down the plug-hole. Maybe it was a bitter divorce or the loss of a job. But when you look back, you see that from the ashes you rose like a phoenix; you met someone who was better suited to you, or you got the push you needed to start your own business, write that book or reignite an old passion.

The bittersweet triumph is only revealed in retrospect; when you recognise it for what it is, however tough the experience, you will be glad that it happened. When you raised your head after the battle, though you may have felt defeated, you looked around at the changed landscape, took what you'd learned and made something of it. A bittersweet triumph.

You won or you learned. Either way, you grew.

Unexpected triumphs

Has an unexpected swerve in your life or work ever taken you down a completely different path to the one you had planned? At one stage of my life I was working as an artist making videos and installations, when I met someone at a party who had just landed a documentary series for Channel 4. She liked my videos and asked if I would be interested in being one of the directors on the series, I said yes and off I went to begin the next chunk of my life, making documentaries.

Perhaps you were on the lookout for opportunities, or maybe you were trundling along minding your own business when a chance meeting, surprise offer or unexpected award or person swept you off your feet. You couldn't believe your good fortune but you grabbed the opportunity and raised your game to a whole new level.

Unexpected triumphs can come out of the blue and shift your life and work. Be sure to share any of the life-changing upward spikes in your roadmap; listeners will love hearing about them and be on the lookout for their own.

The guilty win

Is it ingrained in you to be modest about your wins? Were you told off as a child for 'boasting' or 'showing off'? Have you ever felt guilty when you got a pay rise but your colleagues didn't? Did you feel uncomfortable about becoming cancer-free, when others got sicker or even died? Do you play down your wins because you think no one wants to hear about them, or that you are somehow 'unworthy', or you don't want to come across as bragging?

Celebrate your triumphs and own your wins because listeners will see that when you go after things, you get results and rewards. They want these wins and are listening to find out how you got yours. If you don't dare to share, they can't learn to also pursue and own their achievements.

Epilogue

At the end of the interview, I ask my guests about their vision for the future, because at any given point in time, where you stand is only the end of the story thus far. Tomorrow is another day, the end is the beginning of something new. At the end of films you get a wrap up of the story – the couple get together – and then you get the epilogue, a glimpse of life after the finale – they ride off into the sunset to begin a new adventure together.

If you can leave an interview having inspired, encouraged and empowered listeners to look to their own horizons by painting a picture of yours, you will have gained a fan or potential customer/client. Leave them hungry to hear more and they will catch hold of your tail-wind and follow you wherever you go – other podcasts, on social media, at your events and launches.

Your story is like the pied piper's flute, calling out to and rallying a loyal tribe.

EXAMPLE

Uju Asika[8] is the author of *Bringing Up Race: How to raise a kind child in a prejudiced world*.[9] This was how her story looked:

- **Scene setting:** She experienced racism as a child.
- **Call to action:** She claimed her space in the world as a mum blogger, writer and speaker.
- **The quest:** As a mum and blogger, she helped parents and children to navigate racism.
- **The battle:** She knew she should write a book on parenting and racism but was scared.
- **Her triumph:** Her resolution was that she wrote the book. However, her triumph was bitter-sweet because she finished the book just as the Black Lives Matter movement took off, making it all the more relevant. This aspect of her triumph was unexpected; the world suddenly became more receptive to the subject matter of her book. This might give it an

---

8 L Hamilton, 'Bringing up race: How to raise a kind child in a prejudiced world with author Uju Usika', Brave New Girl (2021), https://podcasts.apple.com/in/podcast/bringing-up-race-how-to-raise-kind-child-in-prejudiced/id1462548683?i=1000492254792
9 Uju Usika, *Bringing Up Race: How to raise a kind child in a prejudiced world* (Sourcebooks, 2021)

aspect of a guilty win – being published at the right time of history created a sense of guilt and imposter syndrome.

- **The epilogue:** She hopes that through communication and education, in the future there will be no need for a book like hers.

Using the structure I've set out, you can shape your life story to fit the classic, simple story framework that guarantees listener satisfaction. The beauty of this basic plot is that you can take any part of your life or work journey and communicate it this way. Perhaps for one podcast you focus on one area or triumph, and for another you find a different relevant part of your story to share.

Learnings

In this section, you have learned how the triumphs in your life and work can have various reflections. You have seen that wins can have many faces, beyond the Oscar, the MBE or the book deal. Dare to share the diversity of your wins alongside all their layers of lessons and deeper meaning. Listeners will be fascinated to hear about them, and curious to look for their own wins and see their life experiences in a new light.

ACTION STEPS

- Write a list outlining what have you won or learned from your battles.

- Describe an event in your life that felt like a failure at the time but, looking back, you can see that things turned out better because of it.

- When has something brilliant happened to you when you least expected it and how did that impact your life or work?

- What wins or triumphs have given you a nagging sense of self-doubt? In two columns, write a) why you felt you were not worthy and b) why you are.

- From where you are right now, what have your wins made you think about your future?

Summary

In this chapter, you learned about why podcasts are a great platform for getting your book, brand, or campaign out into the world, and that storytelling can help to attract podcast listeners and encourage them engage with you beyond the show. I've talked you through the five elements of any good story and explained how to construct a compelling narrative from your life experiences, one that will captivate, engage and inspire podcast listeners. Below, I'll briefly recap each of these elements.

1. Scene-setting

You learned that your story starts somewhere and explored your childhood to set the stage for the road-map of your life. You know that constructing your story is a chance to select from, reflect on and frame the experiences and the events that have shaped you and brought you to this point.

2. Call to action

You learned that all stories can be simplified to the bare bones of a few basic plot lines, and for the purposes of this book we are using the basic hero's journey storyline. Having set the scene, you then identified your call to action, plotted out what your trigger points were and what caused you to take a new direction. You also learned that digging around in your past can be an emotional process and that, while your story is enhanced by 'going deep', you can still hold back in areas you would prefer to keep private.

3. The quest

You learned how to flesh out your quest by breaking it down into elements: the quester (you), an imagined quest, the justification, the challenges and trials, and then the discovery of the real quest. You learned about other people's quests so that you could plot out your own.

4. The battle

There may have been many battles in your life and work, but here you took one and broke it down to understand its parts: the build-up, the frustration stage, the nightmare stage, the battle itself and the aftermath. By walking through this journey, you share with the listeners the hows, the whys and the where-afters of whatever battle you think is most relevant to that podcast.

5. The triumph

You learned about the resolution that comes after a battle, where you have either won or you've learned. You learned that this can be bittersweet – at the time, an event may feel like a failure but in retrospect you see what you've gained from it. It can also be unex-pected, if a big win lands in your lap from out of the blue. It might cause you to feel guilty, if you feel you don't 'deserve' the win – this is just imposter syn-drome causing trouble. Finally, you reach the epi-logue where, with both failures and wins under your belt, you head into the next period of your life.

And there you have it. You have learned how to fit any part of your life or work into a basic story arc that allows you to communicate your experiences and learnings with colour, shape, intrigue, surprise, dark-ness and celebration. Doing this work makes your job as a podcast guest much easier; preparation is every-thing. It also means that you can hop from podcast to podcast with the confidence of knowing that what-ever element or view of your life or work they want to hear about, you can share it in a compelling way through the art of storytelling, with different nuances and/or content for different shows.

TWO

Themes And Topics

This is an exciting chapter where we dive deep into the five points of your story star, helping you to sparkle as the unique you on the airwaves. You will create a storyline around different themes and topics across these five categories, which will enable you to go on different podcasts and offer up a different aspect of yourself on each. Listeners don't mind if some elements are the same when you hop from podcast to podcast, but they love to hear about new things too so it's good to have different themes in your arsenal. These five points are where I take all my guests when they come on my podcast. They take us deep, right to the sweet spots:

- **Passion:** your loves, passions, thrills and gifts

- **Pain points:** what has brought you down, the adversities, challenges and failures

- **Purpose:** why you do what you do, what drives you and gives your life meaning

- **Peaks:** the wins, the highs, the triumphs and trophies

- **Possibilities:** your visions, dreams and hopes for the future

I recommend you tackle one P a day. Put aside an hour each day this week to build your story star. This is the time to really dig deep. After this, the rest of the podcast will be plain sailing. Let's take them one by one.

Passions

Passions are personal. They come in many shapes and sizes. Whatever yours are, it follows that you'll be passionate about talking about them. Listeners love to hear passion in your voice. You'll either have a good line-up of passions to parade on podcasts, or ways to dig deep into your one grand passion so that you can spread the love. Knowing all the potential themes and topics that emerge from your passions will enable you to get onto a wide variety of podcasts.

What is passion? Passion is what makes you jump out of the bed in the morning, fires your soul, is the heart of your book, your brand or your message. When you have a desire that is fuelled by passion, you act upon it. You persevere even when the going gets tough, and you find that you achieve great results. Like fire, sometimes you find that passion burns brightly, other times it dies down to the embers, ready to be fanned up again when you want to come back to it.

You may have one overarching passion or you could be a multi-passioned person. If you have one passion, your challenge will be to find different ways to look at it and talk about it on a podcast to encourage people to follow you across multiple platforms. If you have many passions, you may need to work out a way to streamline them in your storytelling.

Born for it

It's not exactly that your passion is in your DNA, but a combination of access, encouragement and circumstances has paved the way for your passion to blossom from an early age.

Falling in love with your passion is much like falling in love with a person. It hits you full force; you are consumed by it, engulfed in its energy. You want to drown in its power. You feel saved by it. You promise your soul to it. You are ignited by it. You go full throttle, investing money, time, your body and mind. You train in it to go deeper, to learn more, be more, feel more, to grow more into it, through it and from it. Whatever it is, you know it's 'the one' because even when it involves something technical, or boring, or a hard commitment, you are willing and able to keep showing up, day after day, year after year. You are willing to let it make you vulnerable, to risk shame, guilt, fear and failure. You probably experience all of these along the journey and all of the challenges, adversity and setbacks only deepen the passion.

Think about your big passion, or one of them. How did you come to it? How did you fall in love with it, how did it grow and what were the challenges? Think about the journey to now, how your passion has surged, lulled, shifted shape, evolved and transformed. Has there ever been a time when you fell out of love with it? Did you think your passion couldn't be a work thing so you pursued a different career, only to return to your first love later? Have you ever resented its hold on you? Have you at any time branched out into a different area but with the same core passion at its heart?

Big and little fires everywhere

This is where most people find themselves, with maybe one bigger passion but many smouldering away in the background and re-igniting across the landscape of their lives. When you survey your landscape, think about your hierarchy of passions. It can be helpful to think of them as rings of concentric circles, with you at the centre, your most important passions closest to you and those that have less impact on you further away.

As you map out the loves of your life, those big and little fires burning everywhere, jot them down and think about which are suitable themes or topics for podcasts. With over two million podcasts out there (and growing), you can bet your bottom dollar that if you focus on a passion, you'll find a podcast host that will be happy to give you a platform.

Your passion is your superpower

Let's assume that you are fired up to share your passion, your superpower. With passion, you are driven to greater heights than would otherwise be possible. You can deal with anything that life throws at you when you have your passions at heart. Look back at the things that seemed to have tripped you up and follow the trail to your passions; this is where you will find powerful parts of your story.

What were your drivers, either away from or towards something? Think of your passions as the rocket fuel beneath you. Give your list of passions a fuel gauge: 1 is a small force passion, 10 is your superpower passion.

EXAMPLE

I could take any one of my podcast guests and talk about their passion. I encourage you to dip in and listen to the ones that pique your interest and think about their passion and whether they were born for it, fell into it, evolved to find it or have had passions sparking up in various forms throughout their life. Have they used their superpower passion to write a book, build a brand, launch a campaign or overcome a trauma?

I decided I'd better put my money where my mouth is and start guesting on podcasts too. In 'My Story Podcast' hosted by Conrad Weaver, I talk about how art was my passion when I was growing up. I went to art school and spent the following few years creating sculpture commissions before going back to art school to do an

MA in public art. The new technologies of video and audio captured my curiosity and I moved away from art into artist films and then into documentaries with a social slant. My passion had changed form. Over time, the frustrations of trying to get films funded found me losing my sense of creativity. It was only when I faced grief, menopause and an empty nest that I rediscovered my passion for art, started drawing and painting again and unleashed a whole new career as a professional artist, alongside my passion for podcasting and supporting others to voice their passions on podcasts.

How has your passion propelled you?

Learnings

You have learned that passion is the feeling that propels you to take action, to grow something, to nurture it, to keep at it when the going gets tough. It's the backbone to your life and work.

You may have learned that your passion blossomed from a natural gift, something you nurtured and practised from a young age, and then drove all your decisions. It may have evolved and changed over time but it has always been there in some form.

Or, you may have learned that your passion came to you later in life, like falling in a love; an experience of discovery and late blooming, that emerged from living and working and discovering what makes you happy and what doesn't.

You have learned that while you may have one larger passion you can also have many smaller ones burning in the background that fuel your life, health, friendships, work and home in other ways. You have learned that when you fan the flames of passion you can turn it into a superpower that can change your life, or the lives of others, for the better.

It's time now to embed these learnings by taking action.

ACTION STEPS

- Can you define 'passion'?
- Were you born to your passion, or did it blossom later? Draw a wiggly line showing how your passion has played out throughout your storyline.
- Draw a pie chart with eight sections: Home, work, intimate relationships, family, friends, hobbies, travel, culture. Where do the flames of passions flare up in each of these areas?
- How has your passion become your superpower? Think of five ways that your superpower positively impacts your life or those of others.
- Listen to my episode of My Story Podcast and pay particular attention to how my passion evolves over time.[10]

---

10 ConjoStudios, 'Lou Hamilton - How to be fearless', My Story Podcast (2021), https://podcasts.apple.com/us/podcast/lou-hamilton-how-to-be-fearless/id1455872413?i=1000524470185

Pain points

Are you scared of what you might have to share? Those dark times or the messy mistakes that you'd rather bury than broadcast to the world? Remember, you can choose what you dare to share. When you dare share your challenges, adversities, obstacles and pitfalls, you help listeners process their own journey. You will know what you want to be open about and what you'd prefer to keep private.

It doesn't matter if you were born into poverty or with a silver spoon in your mouth, at some point your pie crust breaks and you have to deal with the underbelly, the darker side of life. You may have experienced a single traumatic event, or become overwhelmed by fine layers of sadness that have built on top each other over years. Sometimes, these experiences are so dark that it is hard to see any light emerging from them.

It may have been an extraordinarily painful journey to get to where you are today. If that's the case, you might find that trying to bury the past only has the effect of allowing it to fester deep inside your psyche. When you release it, whether that's through therapy, journaling or turning that pain into power, you can begin to feel hope and perhaps freedom. How you do or have done this is a critical part of your story, the dark night of the soul before the dawn. If you dare to share it, you will show others that it is possible, no matter how bad things get or have been, to emerge from your chrysalis with wings. Podcast listeners will be able to identify with you through your pitfalls, because if you have been through things, grown and learned from them, so can they.

Life interrupted

Few lives are uninterrupted by body blows, break-ups, failures, traumas or disasters. It comes with the territory of being human. We try and do everything we can to prevent it or mitigate pain, but there will usually be something that stops us in our tracks, brings us to our knees, or fells us completely. You will have experienced plenty of pain points, but I want you think about the big one, the one that bulldozed you. If it is not still too painful or raw (in which case, it is not yet the time to share) then lay it out before you in the cold light of day and see it in the context of all that came before and after.

In your journal, draw three circles side by side. In the first circle, write out words that describe life before this pain point. In the middle circle, describe the event itself. In the final circle, describe life afterwards: the lessons you learned about yourself, how you coped, the process of coming out of the storm.

Then go back to the event itself. Describe what happened in as much detail as possible; include colours, smells, feelings, people, places and time. When it comes to describing this experience on a podcast, you don't want it to sound like you've told the story a million times. Including detailed description helps the listener to really hear it. Remember, if it is too painful to recount just yet, you do not need to share it. When you've finished, take a deep breath, give your body a shake and go and do something invigorating and uplifting.

Your story is like a suitcase that you carry with you, adding new things as you travel through life. Do you stuff it with treasures, good memories, happy thoughts, people who treat you well and understand you, dreams and visions for your future? Or, is it heavy baggage that drags you down and holds you back? At any time, you can open up your suitcase, survey what you have collected and decide what you want to do with the contents. Have you been carrying round the pain that others have caused you, or have you replaced painful memories with joyful ones, and more life-affirming people? Your story will always include obstacles. Know that the cracks are what we learn from, they test us, but often through them we find another way ahead.

Starting over

What would happen now if you lost your home, your security, your safety? Would it force you to see your safe place as being within you, an ability to build and rebuild when you are hit by life's knocks? What if you knew that each time the walls of your comfort zone were knocked down you could create another, perhaps bigger than before, because you were braver and stronger and able to take up more space in the world? Not necessarily physically, but mentally, emotionally and spiritually. When you have been though pain and loss, but picked up the pieces, did you feel less fearful about the landslides of life, understanding that this is the geology of living? Knowing that you have survived before and will do so again enables you to grow and adapt in an ever-changing landscape.

If your world has ever fallen apart, how did you start over? What did your heart yearn for, your body crave and your mind need, to heal and thrive? When did you crawl out from your dark space? How did you rebuild? What did you learn? Think about the emotions you felt when starting over.

Vulnerability

How do you feel about opening up to listeners of a podcast? Does it feel scary, or too raw? You don't have to reveal anything you don't want to. If you are going through something right now, it's probably best not to talk about an open wound. With something in your past that you have gained distance from and perspective on, you might be able to be more vulnerable, to reveal those painful moments of loss, heartache, shame or trauma, because now you can see that you survived, even thrived.

Maybe vulnerability means admitting failure or that things didn't go according to plan. It might be that you feel you can talk about one part of a particular experience but keep other aspects private. This is why planning ahead of time is a good idea. Know where you are willing to go and what you are not prepared to share.

EXAMPLE

I interviewed Tamsyn Wood about becoming a carer. Her husband had suffered a brain injury that left him blind, wheelchair-bound and unable to speak. She thought it would be temporary and in the early days clung to hope that he would get better and life would return to normal. Gradually though she came to admit that caring for her husband, advocating for his support and two-to-one care, while raising four young children, was a marathon, not a sprint. She was open about the experience but there were some aspects that she kept to herself. She was in control of the telling of her story; she wasn't afraid to share the emotional fallout while keeping some details private.

Plotting out your story ahead of time gives you the flexibility to decide what will be for public consumption and what won't. This way, you won't be caught out in the middle of an interview with your mouth running off in its own direction, leaving you regretting what comes out.

Learnings

You've learned that if you've been through a dark night of the soul and decide to share the experience, you will help listeners through their own hardships. You've looked at the big bad event and seen it in context, enabling you to describe how you came through it, what you took from it, and how you moved forward.

You've thought about the many pain points you've experienced throughout your life. You can pick and choose from these which are relevant to talk about on different podcasts; they each have a place in your story.

You've looked at how, when the worst happened, you found it in yourself to start again. The ways we find to heal, grow, rebuild or evolve are all helpful bits of wisdom to share.

You've thought about vulnerability and the limits of how far you are prepared to open up in regard to the more sensitive, intimate or painful parts of your tale. Planning ahead is key to feeling in control of what you dare to share.

ACTION STEPS

- Think about why you want to share the tougher times and learning moments. What value do you want to offer?

- What was the big bad event in your life, if you had one? How did you come through it? Complete the circles exercise in the life interrupted section.
- Draw a little wiggly line to plot the pain points along your life journey. How was each one meaningful?
- Draw a vertical line down a page in your journal. On the left, write down the things you don't want to share, and on the right list the painful parts of your story that you are prepared to be vulnerable about.
- Listen to the Tamsyn Wood episode of the BNG podcast.[11]

Purpose

Purpose relates to that one big question: why are we here? Maybe you can't provide an answer for the whole human race, but you can talk about your 'why'. We all know our basic drivers – food, shelter, warmth – but if you are wanting to go on podcasts to talk about something specific, it's likely you have another, higher-level sense of purpose. This section will help you unearth your purpose, your mission, so that you can talk about the driving force behind what you do and why you do it.

Why are we all here – humans, trees, water, stars, the moon? Trying to find answers to these big 'whys' relies

---

11   L Hamilton, 'From true romance to traumatic injury: How to survive as a carer with blogger Tamsyn Wood', Brave New Girl (2021), https://podcasts.apple.com/in/podcast/from-true-romance-to-traumatic-injury-how-to-survive/id1462548683?i=1000494731998

on conjecture and guesswork. It can be a source of fear, crisis or intrigue at the deepest human level, for we do not have the answers. Fortunately, our business here is more straightforward: uncovering our personal whys, our purpose. This is the point on our story star that leads the way. It's up to us to identify these smaller whys in our lives, so that we head out on the right path and then stay on it when the going gets tough.

Beyond the basics of survival, why do you get up in the mornings? What gives your days, your work, your personal endeavours, a sense of meaning? What drives your story forward? Where does the courage come from to enable you to make the choices that will move you closer to your dreams? Where do you thrive?

Perhaps you have struggled to find your purpose, maybe at first you pushed it away. Rather than one clear purpose, yours might have different elements. What topics does your purpose give you to talk about? Brainstorm or journal or mind-map these as they come to you. There is no right or wrong beyond the fact that there is something, or maybe several things, that gets you moving, puts a spring in your step and a whistle in your walk. Even if you haven't found your 'thing' yet, the search is worth talking about, because if you are struggling then you can be sure that there are podcast listeners out there who are too. When they hear you voice your doubts, the pain you've felt on the way to finding your power, they won't feel so alone. In doing this alone, you will have given yourself a purpose.

Frustration

A good way to find your way is to look for your frustrations. Your why might be that you are burned out with the stress of fast-paced modern life, so you set out to live off-grid to make life simpler. What frustrations are you fixing? Your purpose is found in the desire to change what you do not like, to bring to life that which you believe to be important. What is the frustration that has made you seek a different way?

These frustrations aren't always the low hanging fruit. Sometimes you have to look deep to find the one that fires you up, that gives you meaning. As you look at your story for parts to share, you will see patterns within which your whys are woven, often coming after many why nots. When you see what your purpose is and what drives you, what attracts you or what fears you run from, you'll see that it underwrites your story, it is the theme tune to your movie.

Maybe your purpose comes in pieces, crafted from experiences in your life that have moved you to do things differently. Keep journaling as the clues come to you. Shifts in your story may be incremental. Your story is not a straight line, it meanders from one event to the next, one decision to another, but as you look at the map of your life, you will see that what hurt you has transformed you; that where you were once a victim you became a motivator, an inspirer, an innovator, a writer or an activist. What nearly destroyed you, has made you. Your flaws became your strengths. This is the alchemy that makes you who you are and is what gives rise to your mission and purpose. Draw out your road map and note how the different threads slowly weave together until it becomes clear why you do what you do, for whom and for what reason. Be a detective spotting the clues along the way and then, when you have solved the case, you can reveal your conclusion to the listeners.

In a storm, your purpose is the compass that guides you out. It is a way to rewrite your history and find a sense of direction for the present that will take you toward your ideal future. It is the driving force behind all the choices you have made so far. Understanding your whys will give shape to your life story. Sharing your purpose will help others find theirs when they feel lost, heartbroken, discouraged, confused or broken. Let your story be the inspiration that helps them pick up the pieces and carry on. Please, dare to share.

EXAMPLE

Vix Munro was one of my podcast guesting clients, who I placed on many shows with different themes. But underlying the aspects of her story that she shared, her purpose always comes through. Raised in New Zealand, she lost two siblings and her mother when she was eleven and her mother was thirty-five. Vix grew up spending money liberally and living for a good time because she reckoned she wouldn't be living very long. In her early twenties, she arrived in the UK with $30 in her pocket and got into debt as she continued her hedonistic lifestyle. But she entered the corporate world, working in accountancy, economics and pricing. She built a career spanning over thirty years, and ran her own business for the last twelve of those years. When she passed the age that her mother had been when she died, she realised she'd better start planning for the possibility of a long future ahead of her! She built up a portfolio of investments and as she reached her mid-fifties, she finally nailed her purpose. She decided she wanted to help other women entrepreneurs create financial empowerment for themselves so that they can retire rich, whatever that means to them. Vix believes that the balance between having the right mindset and solid financial strategies allows the magic to happen. Her purpose is to support women in finding their financial g-spot and, in so doing, her business Money Badassary was born.

Learnings

You have learned that purpose is the 'why' that drives you to succeed, to survive and thrive. You have learned that it can drive you away from something painful and toward something good; that it is your call to action, and that through every knock-back and failure, it is what helps you get back on your feet again. It may have come to you in single threads throughout different stages of your life but, looking back, you can see how those threads have been woven together to create your purpose, your reason for moving forwards. Sharing your whys, your overall purpose and mission statement will help podcast listeners to see where the jet fuel that has driven your achievements has come from.

ACTION STEPS

- List the painful things that you have been driven away from.
- List the good things that you have been driven towards.
- Write out your core 'why' in the middle of the page and, fanning out from it, write your smaller whys.
- Craft your mission statement from these whys.
- Listen to the Vix Munro episode on Melitta Campbell's podcast The Female Driven Entrepreneur.[12]
- And on the BNG podcast.[13]

Peaks

Listeners want to hear about your wins, your triumphs, your stories of overcoming adversity and being rewarded for your deeds. As a listener, it is reassuring to hear someone do this, as it gives us permission to celebrate the good moments in our own lives.

---

12 M Campbell, 'Retiring rich for female entrepreneurs: Vix Munro', Brave New Girl (2020), https://podcasts.apple.com/gb/podcast/60-retiring-rich-for-female-entrepreneurs-vix-munro/id1502412440?i=1000517214645

13 L Hamilton, 'Finding your financial G-spot when you're in a money muddle, with Vix Munro', Brave New Girl (2020), https://podcasts.apple.com/in/podcast/finding-your-financial-g-spot-when-youre-in-money-muddle/id1462548683?i=1000511370893

In the triumph section of the storytime chapter we looked at your wins. Now we are going to dig deeper into these, to give you even more to share.

The only time life flatlines is when we are dead. Until then, we are on a perpetual rollercoaster of peaks and troughs. The pain points often galvanise us, give us a chance to recalibrate, or make shifts we've long avoided. The peaks are the wins, the moments when we emerge triumphant, having taken the blows, overcome adversity, conquered challenges, moved mountains and stood on the podium of reward, award, applause and success. It is tempting in these moments to say, 'I've made it', but as with the dips and darker times, these peaks too shall pass. The rhythm is best embraced as a state in flux: you win some, you lose some. You stumble and you soar.

The peaks are the good times. Although we tend to remember or ruminate over the hard times, it is important to acknowledge and celebrate the wins, both big and small. All stories come with ups and downs, so tell us about both when you share yours. Step up to the mic to bring us your wins.

There is a time and a place for modesty. Perhaps you were raised not to 'boast' or your elders told you, 'No one likes a show-off'. That conditioning is hard to shake. In some contexts it's appropriate; when someone comes along thumping their chest and shouting about their success or the big bucks they earn or flouting their amazing house/holiday/partner, it lands awkwardly. But when we've heard about your lows, traumas and challenges, sharing your wins, triumphs and lessons learned gives hope and redemption to your story. We know the context, we understand where you came from and it is helpful to understand the balance between the dark and the light.

Golden moments and quiet moments

We all love the heroic wins, the podium moments, the recognition from the Queen or awards from Hollywood. We relish those stories because they remind us of the fairy tales we heard as children. Whether it's the rags to riches story, the heroine winning the battle, or she who dares wins, our eagerness to hear about triumph over adversity comes from our need to make sense of the world. If things are tough but we work hard, we will reach paradise. This is the narrative we all play out in our minds. Of course, we don't all get an Olympic medal, an Oscar or an OBE, but most of us have our big moments. What were your triumphs, the golden moments that you look back on and can hardly believe they happened to you, or that you made happen? Wow us with your wins.

Of course, it's all well and dandy celebrating these big triumphs; they are relatively rare, so make hay while the sun shines. But life isn't always flush with golden moments, and they are rarely where contentment is found. It feels like magic when we experience these major peaks, but the euphoria fades quickly. Long-lasting satisfaction is in the gentle drift at the end of the day when you realise you have made real progress. Or when, from a deep depression, you climb out of bed and get dressed. Or in the hug from a child who knows you are the shelter from their storm.

What have been your quiet moments of triumph? Maybe it was the moment you realised you were ready to write your book. Or when you found courage in a situation you had no control over, when you put one foot in front of the other and took the next step. That step was a win.

Overcoming adversity

The transition through dark times is where you find your strength and resilience, and there is comfort in knowing you can survive. Sometimes, the experience may feel transformative. You learn what is truly important to you, how you want to spend your time, who you want to be with. You know more about yourself, your values and your vision for the future.

When have you experienced this kind of transition and transformation and how has it played out in your story?

EXAMPLE

Karen Arthur, one of my guests on the BNG podcast, was a teacher for decades. She loved her work and was good at it, putting her heart and soul into it every waking hour, until her body couldn't take it anymore. One day, during a fire drill, instead of going to stand outside with the rest of the school, she picked up her belongings and went home and wept. A friend urged her to seek help, and she did. She was having a breakdown. It took time, therapy, a good friend and trust in herself, but she came through. Looking back, she realised it wasn't a breakdown but a breakthrough. She wanted to live a creative life so she went back to her passion for sewing and began to make clothes and teach sewing classes. At the same time, she was going through the menopause and found that, for black women, this change wasn't spoken about or reflected anywhere she looked for help. She decided to be the advocate and fact-gatherer for women like her and, in doing so, she found her purpose. The peaks have been plentiful after her breakthrough, not least in finding herself.

Karen's story had its pitfalls, but after them came peaks, once she rediscovered her passion and found her purpose.

Learnings

You've learned that peaks can take many shapes. You know that sharing your good times is not boasting when they are set within the context of your life story. You know that it is important to celebrate those golden moments and that they give listeners hope, but you also know that a peak needn't be a trophy or an award, it can just as easily be the ability to smell the roses on a hard day. You know that when you come through dark times and experience the transformative feeling of having overcome adversity, challenges or difficult times, these are peaks worth sharing so that others can benefit from the lessons they taught and the hope they inspire.

ACTION STEPS

- Brainstorm the peaks in your story.
- If something feels like boasting, think about how you can reframe it as a consequence of previous action, effort or luck.
- Draw a podium and draw yourself holding a trophy. What is your trophy for? You are giving this to yourself. What are your golden moments to treasure?
- And what are the quieter moments, the 'Aha' moments, the daily peaks or pleasures?
- Listen to Karen Arthur's story on BNG and then describe your own transformative experiences.[14]

Possibilities

Does it feel as though talking about the future is tempting fate? On the contrary, declaring your goals, intentions, dreams and vision for the future and how you intend to get there makes you more closely

14   L Hamilton, 'Breaking through depression & menopause to wearing your happy with fashion designer Karen Arthur', Brave New Girl (2020), https://podcasts.apple.com/in/podcast/breaking-through-depression-menopause-to-wearing-your/id1462548683?i=1000488633833

aligned to that goal. Podcasters love to know about the possibilities for your future, both personally and professionally. After working through this section, you will know what you want to share about your vision for the future.

Of the five points of your story star, you have so far discovered what your passions are, what fires you up and makes you curious. You then saw how your pitfalls, challenges and failures have given you a backbone, made you stronger, forced you to dig deeper and reach further, and you have also identified your purpose, what it is that drives you and fuels your flames. You have acknowledged that the peaks and wins of your life story have manifested in many forms. Finally, we come to the possibilities in your story; this is about the next stage of your journey, from where you are now to where you are going next.

With what you know about your journey so far, what do you project for your future? What dreams do you still hope to fulfil, what mountains are next to climb? When you listen to podcasts, the guests often talk about where they are going next. We are a transitory species; we aren't an end point, the sum of our story thus far, content to stay where we've landed. We also exist in our imaginations, in our forward thinking, with a curiosity and hunger for more. All our stories end in a coffin. Until then, we are a work-in-progress, a story we are still drafting, editing, re-writing and inventing as we go along.

When you have been through frustrations, challenges and dark times and you are starting to find your feet again, your imagination will find space to fast forward. Thinking about the coronavirus crisis, did you ever imagine yourself walking back out into a post-apocalyptic world, blinking into the sunlight, dazzled by the growing buzz of people pouring out of their houses and back into the bustle of everyday existence? Whenever troubling times come to an end, you can find yourself reassessing. You know what is important to you, and you'll find yourself pointing in the direction of your true north.

From fact to fiction

When you're recounting events that took place in the past, your story is non-fiction. You relay what happened, how you felt, what it meant for you. The future is where fact becomes fiction and you become a different kind of storyteller. This storytelling involves a re-imagining of the past to create future possible landscapes, reshuffling the cards and laying them out like a tarot reader. You get to bring ideas, concepts and visions out of your head and introduce them to the minds of others. You can influence, inspire and impact them. Whoever you are, in guesting on podcasts, you can give voice to your opinions, actions and world re-ordering. You get to carve out the future through your words and ideas.

You may think you have a small voice, that you are taking small actions, but consider the butterfly effect.

What you choose to do moving forward will undoubtedly have impact. Each shimmer of good intention causes a ripple across the world. From one human to another, we give each other hope. As we join forces, so begins the movement of minds. Your voice matters, your opinions count, your actions stir others to make the effort. Your beating butterfly wings will pound the airwaves and the reverberations will carry far and wide, reaching hundreds and thousands of people.

You simply have to show up with your intentions, wisdom, expertise and vision. You have to be bold and believe that your story matters. You have to be brave and speak your truth. You must have the courage to step up and project your possibilities for the future. The technology is there, the platform is there, the listeners are waiting. Imagine the effect of your words, of your vision for the future, as you unleash them out into the world. How many people will sit up and take notice and decide to make a change in their own lives?

Crystal vision

When you have absolute clarity, a crystal vision of what you want for your future and a clear strategy for getting there, you're more likely to reach your destination. Like a road trip, you know where you are heading and you have a map to help you navigate the route. That's not to say that nothing will get in your way. Perhaps there are roadworks and you have to change route. What you don't do is say, 'Oh well, I won't go to X after all.' You look at the map, adjust your route and continue. With a crystal vision and strategy, you may hit challenges along the way but by being prepared to be flexible, you can continue on your journey to reaching your goal.

When you share your vision on podcasts, make it crystal clear. Paint a vivid picture and bring it to life with colour and flourishes. Get excited about the details. Talk about it in the present tense so the listeners feel like they are living it as you speak. Tell them how you're getting there. When your vision is clear, listeners may find their own clarity.

EXAMPLE

Hannah Turner told BNG about a time when her business coach asked her where she wanted to be in five years' time. 'Retired' popped out of her mouth and she laughed, but the coach was serious and replied 'OK, well let's work toward that'. Hannah was startled. 'Really, we can do that?' she asked. 'Of course. If that's where you set your intention, then that's where you'll be heading.' And so they hatched a plan. Hannah would start the process of archiving designs for the future. Instead of creating a design for her ceramics and homeware range and putting it into production straightaway, she would store it ready to be used by someone in the future to keep the brand going. This meant that Hannah wouldn't have to work 'in' the business indefinitely, but that even without her, the brand would continue with her style and images. That paved the way for Hannah's vision of retirement.

Learnings

You can see now what your possibilities are. You know that coming out of troubling times is the perfect opportunity to reassess and look forward. You understand that future-telling is storytelling and that your stories will help others with their own forecasts. You know that writing your stars will help create a constellation of other vivid futures; in this way, you will have a ripple effect. You understand that by having a crystal vision and clear route to reaching it makes you more likely to turn that vision into reality. This is a message worth sharing.

ACTION STEPS

- Sit still somewhere quiet. Think about where you are right now, the lessons you've learned and the parts of your life that you love.

- What qualities of life do you want for your future? What values do you uphold?

- Write out a detailed, descriptive paragraph of your vision for the future.

- Create a mind-map of how you intend to make your vision happen. This will be your road map.

- Listen to the Hannah Turner episode of the BNG podcast.[15]

---

15 L Hamilton, 'Crockery, creatures, creativity & conservation with ceramicist Hannah Turner', Brave New Girl (2021), https://podcasts.apple.com/in/podcast/crockery-creatures-creativity-conservation-ceramicist/id1462548683?i=1000496294178

Summary

Well done on working through your themes and top-ics. This is the hardest part done. You've dug deep and you will the reap rewards. You have mined for all your gold and will know what themes and topics to focus on when you start to research podcasts to pitch to. For each, you can cast your eye back over your notes to pull out unique gems that will resonate with their listeners. Let's remind ourselves what we learned in this chapter.

1. Passion

Passion is the fire within that propels you to take action, to grow something, to nurture it, to keep at it when the going gets tough. It is the backbone to your life and work. When you fan the flames of your passion it can become a superpower that can change your life, or those of others, for the better. Sharing your passions on podcasts encourages listeners to look for their own, bring them to the fore and be spurred on to live life with passion in their heart.

2. Pain points

It's a rare life that isn't derailed occasionally. We all bear the scars of a life battle fought somewhere along the line, whether it was a juggernaut or simply the occasional challenge. Big or small, these pitfalls lead to resilience and growth. Sharing how you survived them and picked yourself back up will help listeners to feel they aren't the only ones facing headwinds, storms and shipwrecks.

3. Purpose

Your purpose is your rocket fuel. It drives you toward your dreams and goals, brings focus and gives your life and work a sense of meaning. When times are tough, your purpose fires you on. When you face a crossroads or decision, you look to your purpose to find the road that keeps you in alignment with your goals. How you discovered your purpose, how you nurtured it and how you use it are all parts of your story that are interesting to hear about. Tell the listeners about your whys.

4. Peaks

Tell people about your wins. Podcast listeners aren't ambulance chasers only interested in your sorrows, losses and blow-outs. Hearing about how you reached the top of a particular mountain, overcame adversity or found hope in the smallest of things, gives listeners permission to acknowledge their own triumphs. When you show gratitude for your successes, others can feel thankful for the things that have gone right for them too.

5. Possibilities

Paint the listeners a picture from where you stand right now, with everything you have learned, lost, won, celebrated and mastered to date – with your eyes on the horizon, what do you see? What is the crystal vision that you imagine for your future? What are your new goals, dreams and hopes? Do you have a strategy for getting there? Your ideas will trigger thoughts of their own for listeners; you daring to share what your future could look like will give them permission to seek clarity on theirs.

Overview

Digging deep into all the themes and topics of your overarching life story will help you find a breadth of podcasts to pitch to. And when you are booked as a guest on a variety of shows you won't have to tell the same tale each time. You will have layers of experience to reveal and many anecdotes to dip into so that you can always offer something new and unique to the listeners. This will enable you to build up a tribe of new listeners and followers as you tour the airwaves, but you will also deepen the trust and loyalty of those who had already found you and want to continue following your journey and learning from your experiences.

Be a guiding light, fill the world with your inspiring voice, courage and tenacity. Give the world your all.

PART 2
GUESTING ON PODCASTS

WE ALL RISE BY LIFTING OTHERS

THREE
Pitch Perfect

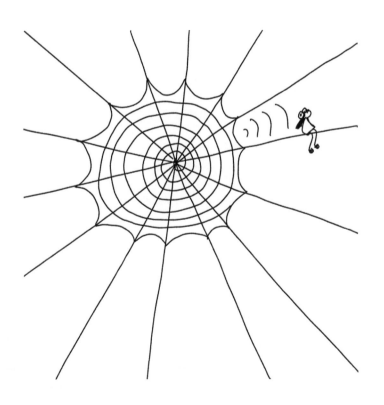

Now you have identified your overarching story and its underlying themes and topics, you are able to go and search out the podcasts that are relevant to you. Part two of this book will help you identify those podcasts, pitch to them and secure a place on their waiting list. This is a numbers game so don't be disheartened when you get rejections; it might be that the podcaster's list is full for the foreseeable future, or that your story isn't quite what they are looking for right now. The podcasts that are right for you are the ones that will say yes. But first you need to get in front of the gatekeepers.

In this chapter, you will learn how to research relevant podcasts, send them a winning pitch and set yourself up for success. We will cover:

- What podcasters want

- Researching podcasts

- How to pitch

- Spreading your net

- Your worth

There are well over two million podcasts and rising (2021), so there will be plenty that are relevant to you. Your job is to find them and explain why you are perfectly mission-matched, giving them reasons to say yes.

What podcasters want

In this section, we'll get into the mindset of a podcaster so that your approach to pitching is based on an in-depth knowledge of their show. Understanding what a host wants to achieve in their podcast and being able to show you fit within their remit demonstrates to them that you have done your research. You want them to know that you have listened to multiple episodes, analysed who their guests are and what subject matter they cover; that you know what kind of message they are trying to send out to the world; that you know who their listeners are and what they want to gain from the show; and that you understand the format and what the guest brings to the table.

If you can understand all these elements of the show, you can pitch in a way that shows the host you are the right kind of guest. As a podcast host myself, I am pitched often. The successful pitches are the ones where the potential guest tells me what they understand the show to be and why they would be a good fit. If I get the sense that all they are interested in is touting their wares, then it's a no. If they tell me how their story aligns with the podcast's DNA and how their contribution will help the listeners, I invite them on the show.

Podcasters carefully curate their shows so if you can persuade them that you'll provide exactly what they are after, and with an added bit of sparkle, then you are in with a chance. Hosts often have guests lined up long in advance, so don't be disheartened to be put on their waitlist – that's better than rejection.

Understanding a podcast's DNA

When you first approach the host you'll need a short summary of your story, tailored to fit with their show's format and themes. It sounds glib, but make sure you study the shows of the podcasters you are pitching to – I know from making this mistake myself. I once pitched to a podcast that focused on grief, which unfortunately I have a lot of experience of. I was pleased with the pitch. Then I listened properly to the show (wrong way round) and realised that the host only invited comedians to talk about grief. I'm not a comedian. I've not made that mistake again and now I'm urging you: become fully acquainted with the show's identity and then explain why you are a good fit.

To do this, you need to listen closely and intentionally to the show. Listen to at least three episodes, so you are completely au fait with the host's interview style and the kinds of guests they bring on. As you listen to the episodes, write down the answers to these questions:

- What is their format; is it formal or conversational?

- What kinds of questions do they ask?

- How long are the episodes?

- Who are the other guests?

- Are you genuinely the right guest for the show? If so, why?

- What themes and topics can you bring to the table?

Who are the listeners?

The person on the other side of the airwaves is something that many guests and hosts fail to drill down on. This relates to the partnership element of podcast guesting. You and the host are exposing each other to your respective tribes in the hope of attracting more people to your platform, book, brand, service, product and so on. But you need the right kind of people. There is no point in approaching a podcast host whose demographic is young males aged twenty-five to thirty-five who are into drinking and comedy, if you are promoting a book about menopause. Ideally, the host's audience won't be exactly the same as yours but they do need to be complementary or related. For instance, continuing the same example product, if the host's listeners are women in their forties, while most of them won't have reached menopause yet, they may unwittingly be experiencing peri-menopausal symptoms, and your advice will also help those in the run-up to it.

Understanding who the listeners of the show are will help you target your messaging. What do they want to learn, and what can you teach them? If you can mission-match, point this out to the host when you submit your pitch. They will appreciate that you have done your homework and are thinking of their gain as well as your own.

What about reach?

You need to be pitching to hosts whose podcasts are roughly within your 'reach range'. You may have to go on lots of shows whose reach is less than yours, just to get some under your belt, but then you can start to push that reach, as you'll be better at targeting, pitching and guesting.

Working out a podcast's reach is a dark art. Currently, there is no search engine that will give you exact analytics on a podcast's reach in the way that you can understand your own, though there are a few places emerging that can give you an idea. That said, also consider that people may listen but not download. A podcast may not have high listener numbers but could be precisely targeted at a unique audience and so have high engagement and loyalty. Ratings and reviews help to understand who listens and what they like or dislike about a show. More crucial than numbers is whether the listeners could potentially become your fans and followers, clients or customers: fifty interested listeners is better than a thousand unaligned ones.

EXAMPLE

The jewellers Astrid and Miyu have a podcast called After Hours, the guests on which are inspirational women chatting through everyday topics over a good old gossip, as well as more business-focused themes, telling the stories of how founders of established brands got to where they are today. I pitched Emily Syphas, founder of Sober and Social, a community established to support those starting or already on their sober journey who still wanted to be able to party, just without alcohol. Her background was in working for a nightlife concierge service, so she was the ideal guest for After Hours, talking about how to have fun without booze, and also about how she was building her brand. She was just the type of guest Astrid and Miyu were looking for.[16]

Learnings

You have learned to identify what a podcast host is looking for, and how to make sure that your story aligns with its DNA and that what you have to say is what the listeners want to hear. You do this by doing

---

16 Astrid and Miyu, 'Social sobriety with Emily Syphas', After Hours S2 EP3 (2019), https://podcasts.apple.com/gb/podcast/after-hours-s2-ep3-social-sobriety-with-emily-syphas/id1479054355?i=1000468758454

your homework on the show to understand its format, themes and typical guests. You have worked out who their listeners are and the reach of the show and know that these roughly match your own. But you also know you can punch above your weight if you have a good enough pitch and can also guest on a show with a smaller following if you can see that it has high engagement. Remember that, over time, a podcast will grow and your episode will continue attracting listeners (and fans).

In summary, you know how to give a podcast host excellent reasons to book you for one of their sought-after slots.

ACTION STEPS

Create a questionnaire around your learnings in this section, with questions to answer about each podcast you wish to approach. Then choose a podcast and practise completing the questionnaire. Suggested questions would be:

- Who are the podcast's listeners and what does the host want to give them?
- What is the podcast's DNA, and what can you bring?
- What is the format of the show, type of questions and typical guests?
- Is the podcast still current or has it pod-faded (a term for when a podcast ceases to air)?
- What is the reach and engagement of the show?

- Complete this questionnaire for every show before you pitch the host. It will soon become second nature to analyse it in this way.

Researching podcasts

With so many podcasts out there, how do you find the ones that are right for you? It's all about finding the right method and applying it consistently over time. By the end of this section, you will have a list of podcasts to listen to and will know what information to take away from them. I can't stress enough that you must listen to the podcasts. There is no shortcut.

Themes

Look for potential themes and topics that you can weave into your story. This helps you increase the scope of the type of podcasts you can guest on. Go back and read your story notes to help you with this. Think about:

- What themes relate to your passion/s? For example, health, creativity, self-development.

- What themes relate to your pitfalls? For example, mental health issues, finding courage through adversity, alcoholism and sobriety, grief, divorce.

- What themes relate to your purpose? For example, promoting diversity, saving the planet, creating a happy place.

- What themes relate to your peaks? For example, achieving goals, understanding success, learning a mindful approach.

- What themes relate to your possibilities? For example, rewilding the countryside, building a global community, leaving the corporate world.

Try and list as many alternative themes as you can; aim for 50. I know that's a lot, but it will stretch you to be more imaginative about all the different things you could talk about, giving you so much more scope for your pitches.

Categories

Next, pick a theme from your list. Let's say your passion relates to the theme of helping female entrepreneurs look after their money and build a wealthy retirement. The categories of podcasts that you could search for might include business, female entrepreneurs, money and wealth management. There are a number of free or subscription-based apps you can use to research podcasts. Whatever you use, go to the categories and select business. Under this heading you might have careers, entrepreneurship, investing, management, marketing and non-profit. I would start with entrepreneurship or investing. Pick one and begin searching through. There will likely be thousands to choose from, which can feel overwhelming.

If your social reach is around a thousand followers, begin by picking out the podcasts that are roughly in your reach range. This doesn't have to be exact, but it gives you a margin to narrow your search. Remember that the listening or ratings figures don't always reflect actual downloads, which may be much higher, or the strength of listener engagement, so if a podcast leaps out at you but the numbers don't match yours, dive in for a deeper investigation. You can either make a longlist and then go back to dig deeper, or do this one at a time. I prefer to do the latter, so that I can rule out a podcast quickly if it's not right, and if it does look like it might be a goer, I'll find out more about it.

Mission-matching

Next, read the details of the show. This tells you what it is about, what it aims to do, and who it intends to reach. It's like looking for a job. You read the job spec and think, 'Yes, that sounds interesting to me and I think I can bring something to the table.' The next thing to check is that the podcast does have guests and isn't simply a teaching podcast with the host as the lone voice throughout the series. If so, this obviously is not a platform for you. If they do have guests, then this is the time to listen to at least three episodes. Again, think about your themes and topics. Be honest with yourself: would you be a good guest? What would be your angle? What are you offering their listeners? How does what you have to share fit with the show's DNA?

As well as working through your questionnaire from the last section, make notes on what you liked about the three episodes, the guests, the host's questions and approach. Were they funny, inspirational, thought-provoking? How did it affect you? What did you learn? How would you have answered the questions?

Making contact

Some hosts are easy to connect with and leave their email address in the show notes or on their website. They invite you to approach them and reach out. Others may have various gatekeepers to avoid being swamped in an avalanche of enquiries and pitches that have no relevance to their show. There might be a form on the website to fill in. Or you might have to go through the host's agent, or find them and direct message them on social media or pay for podcast search engines which find the email for you. One way or another, there will be a way to contact the host, but it might not be straightforward. This means that when you do get your message in front of them, you need to deliver exactly what they are after – or something even better. We'll go into this in more detail in the pitching section. For now, your mission is to find that email address, website form or social media link.

Your assets

Your assets are what the podcaster will use to promote your episode, should they have you on as a guest. This will generally be your biography and a portrait photo of you, ideally with some kind of context of what it is that you do.

Look at the photos used by podcasters you are going to pitch to. Do they add their own logos to the photos of their guests? Do they tend to use a portrait picture rather than landscape? Make sure you provide a high-resolution photograph, preferably taken by a professional. Add it to your one-sheet biography, but be prepared to send it separately if you get on the show.

The other asset you need to provide is your biography. This is a bit like a CV but distilled into a few paragraphs, summarising your career journey and your wins. This is your chance to mention that you are a bestselling author, an award-winning scientist, a gold Olympic champion or an MBE – only if you are, of course. Look back over your peaks and include some of the most relevant. This is the time to blow your own trumpet. It is likely that, if they choose you to be a guest, the podcaster will use parts of this biography in their promotion materials, so make it interesting. Send it as a Word document so that they can simply cut and paste relevant sections, and write in the third person: 'she/ he' rather than 'I'.

Once you've written it, look back over your biography – if you read it, would you want to listen to forty or so minutes of this person? It should draw listeners in. Look at the show notes of other guests that have appeared on the show. How are their bios written, what are the highlights? Your biography is not the pitch itself, but attached to the pitch email as back up information.

EXAMPLE

Here is the biography of one of my podcast guest agency clients.

Dawn McGruer

Dawn always did things differently. Extremely bright with a creative flare, she didn't thrive in the confines of school. She left but found her own way to continue her studies while taking the world of work by storm. But by twenty-one she was done with corporate life. Six deaths in so many months made her reassess how she wanted to live. Success had come easily, yet she felt unfulfilled. When she stepped into entrepreneurship, positively impacting the lives of others through dynamic digital marketing training, she knew she'd found her path.

Dawn's mission is to inspire entrepreneurs to rise to meet today's challenges and be powerfully present to shine online. She is the founder of Business Consort, a CIM-accredited digital and social media academy (www.digitalandsocialmediaacademy.com). She trained and certified upwards of 28,000 specialists in the field and enjoyed fourteen years of success.

She is host of 'Dawn of a new era – The Chronicles of a Serial Entrepreneur' podcast,[17] a business and

---

17 D McGruer, Dawn of a New Era Podcast, (2021), https://podcasts. apple.com/gb/podcast/dawn-new-era-podcast-entrepreneur-dawn-mcgruer-marketing/id1523298824

marketing podcast with a difference, which regularly reaches the top 5% of podcasts globally. Every week she shares her real life experiences and stories as an entrepreneur: the good, the bad and the ugly, along with the pains, problems and pitfalls she and her guests have faced as business owners.

Dawn is an award-winning speaker and strategist, and bestselling author of *Dynamic Digital Marketing*, with over five million subscribers. She was named 'Best Female Speaker' at the Professional Speaker Awards. Her Dynamic Digital Marketing Model was named Solution Framework of the Year. Her insights are in high demand, and her expertise and experience has been rewarded with lifetime Fellowships with the RSA (Royal Society of Arts, Manufactures and Commerce) and CIM. Dawn has a strong online presence including ranking in the top 1% globally on LinkedIn as well as boasting an enviable five million-strong subscriber base, which proves she has the credentials to lead others to digital marketing success.[18]

Don't compare your achievements to Dawn's; just look at the timeline, the peaks and the mission. Now write yours with this in mind.

---

18 N Lloyd, 'Dawn McGruer - Entrepreneur since age 21; freedom, adventure and making connections', Beehive Household, (2021), https://podcasts.apple.com/gb/podcast/dawn-mcgruer-entrepreneur-since-age-21-freedom-adventure/id1538726945?i=1000521375766

Learnings

You now have a list of your themes and topics. You know how to search podcast categories that cover your areas of interest, how to find sub-categories and home in on the podcasts that match your criteria, reach and mission. Now your focus is on the podcasts you have narrowed your search to. You know how to listen for the key elements in any podcast: the types of questions, the format, the guests, the DNA of the show. Once you feel confident that you are the kind of guest the podcast host is looking for, you know how to find their contact details and submit your pitch. You know how to write a good biography and the kind of photograph you need to provide; you understand what the podcaster needs from these assets because you have looked at the show notes of other guests.

ACTION STEPS

You have been taking action throughout this lesson, so just to make sure you have ticked all these tasks off, here's a recap of the action steps:

- List the themes you can cover under these headings: passion, pitfalls, purpose, peaks and possibilities.
- Search for relevant podcast categories on Cast Box, Listen Notes or similar.
- Choose a podcast and analyse its DNA. Do you fit its criteria?
- Find the podcaster's contact details.
- Create your assets: your biography and profile photo.

How to pitch

Now you've done your research, it's time to actually reach out. But what if they say no? They might, but what if they say yes? Simply follow the steps in this section and make your pitch. Then do another and another. You will soon come to know what to pitch, what works and what doesn't. This is your chance to catch the podcast host's attention. If you follow these steps, you will nail your pitch. You'll also know how to deal with the waves of emotions and your inner critic.

Preparation

You've done your research. You've chosen a theme, searched for the right category, found a podcast that looks like it matches your mission, it is still current and has roughly the right reach. You've listened to at least three episodes and made notes. You know how your story could fit into the series. You have got the contact address and have your biography and profile photo at the ready.

Well done, you've prepared. You are good to go.

Just do it

I know how nerve-wracking pitching can be. You've got heart palpitations, your mind is racing with self-sabotage and inner voices telling you you're not right for the show. Why would they want little old you?

They probably have a waitlist from here to Timbuktu. Who are you to tell them how great you are? Who even cares anyway?

Stop. Let the podcast host decide whether or not you are right for the show. All you need to do is give them the evidence, set the ball in motion and you've done your job. Tell them why you love their podcast and a specific guest in particular, and not just the most recent; show you've looked through their whole back catalogue by choosing an old episode that particularly resonates for you. In a couple of sentences explain who you are and what you do. Outline your credentials and mention three themes or topics you could offer – be specific in how your contribution will add to their show and their listeners. Show your social footprint and attach your biography and headshot. Include hyperlinks to your website, your own podcast, socials and recent podcast appearances. (I've provided a template in the example at the end of this section.)

Read and reread your pitch email, check for typos and press send.

Save it

Create a system for tracking your pitch submissions and replies. I use a running spreadsheet with: podcast name, podcast host, contact details, their social reach, date of submission, success or rejection, date for recording, date for release. I am not normally a spreadsheet kind of gal but there is value in this. With this kind of system, you will have an overview of your progress and won't submit to the same podcast twice. The exception to this is if you massively increase your reach, bring out something new, have an exhibition coming up, a rebrand or a new product. Or you might have a life experience that is more relevant to the subject matter of their show. Then, you can submit again.

You should always tweak your pitch according to the podcast and should never send the exact same email for multiple podcasts, but it's useful to cut and paste the elements of the pitch that stay roughly the same from one submission to the next. One word of warning on cutting and pasting: I received a pitch that started out promisingly, until I read 'I particularly loved your podcast...' followed by the name of someone else's podcast. When you copy and paste, be careful and proofread.

Don't hold your breath

You're excited, you've taken the time to put together a great pitch and you're convinced you'll soon be in the hot seat with your favourite podcast host. But time ticks by and you've not heard a dicky bird, and that's not for lack of checking your emails. You go back and look at the pitch letter – did you miss something out?

Could you have worded it differently? Did it make you sound like a show-off, or too boring?

You are attempting to control the outcome, but all you can do is what you have already done: solid research, mission-matching, strong pitching. Whether or not the host will recognise your suitability for their show is not in your power. You might not be what they are looking for right now, or they might be fully booked for the foreseeable future.

Or, you might get a no. You simply might not be their cup of tea. If it's a no, it's more likely that you won't hear anything. Rejection doesn't feel good. Someone has decided you're not right for the show, which you interpret as not good enough for any show. They say their waitlist is full and you take that as your failure to cut the mustard. The point is, for whatever reason, you are not right for them. Make a note on your spreadsheet that you were not accepted for this show and move on.

You will be someone else's cup of tea. Remember, there are millions of podcasts. There will be some who think you are just the voice they are looking for. It's a numbers game, you just have to keep pitching. It's the same as applying for jobs or trying to get press.

It takes gumption, perseverance and tenacity. You've got this.

EXAMPLE

I have developed this pitch template inspired by ideas from Business Coach Megan Accardo (www.meganaccardo.com/work). All you have to do is fill in the blanks.

Dear X,

I discovered your podcast recently and [*say why you enjoyed it*]! It's a great message to be sharing with the world [*give a reason*]! I loved [*episode*], because [*give reason*] which is so important because [*reason*]. [*If you have a personal connection or been impacted in some way, add a one-liner here.*]

If you are looking for other guests, I'd love to pitch myself with [*insert relevant topic*], for your consideration.

[*Put your highest achievements here: eg millionaire of your own making, award-winning speaker, bestselling author of 'xxxx', social footprint, credentials, expertise etc.*]

I'm sure you are regularly pitched by potential podcast guests, but I hope this is of interest to you, as I try to pitch to podcasts that are truly aligned with my purpose, vision and values.

Some interesting themes and topics that I could bring to the conversation could be:

1.

2.

3.

If you would be interested in having a call or you have any questions, please do let me know. I'm attaching my biography for more information.

Recent podcast appearances [*give hyperlink*]

Website [*hyperlink*]

Socials [*hyperlink*]

I feel I can offer you and your listeners an inspiring, informative and entertaining episode, and I will share and help promote your podcast.

Thank you so much for your consideration.

Learnings

In this section, you have learned how to prepare, how not to procrastinate and how to overcome the self-sabotaging inner voice. You've learned what to pitch and how to communicate to the podcast host that what you have to offer is a perfect fit for the ethos of their show. You've learned how to create a system to store all the contact you've had with podcast hosts so that you have an overview of who you have pitched to, and whether they said yay or nay. You know that you may get rejected, or not hear back at all, but you understand that that is part of the process and that you just need to get back on the horse and try again.

ACTION STEPS

- Prepare by listening again to your target podcast and make notes on the format, question types, guests and DNA of the show.

- Write your pitch letter, attach your biography and profile photo.
- Create a system to log who you submit to and whether you were accepted or rejected.
- Keep building your email list and growing your audience and expertise. What one thing can you do this week to progress in each of these areas?
- List your self-sabotaging thoughts and comments and, in a parallel column, provide a response from your voice of reason. Always counteract your inner fear with outer courage, built on past evidence.

Spreading your net

Will people not get bored of what you have to say as you go from one podcast to the next? No, because you're going to spread your net across a variety of genres and topics so your story will never get boring. Get one podcast under your belt and see if you like the experience; if you do, keep going. You've learned the process of pitching, now you'll learn how to spread your net far and wide.

As a marketing strategy, podcast guesting is dynamite. You get to spend forty or so minutes chatting about 'your thing' and can reach millions of people across the globe, one podcast at a time. This is the point of serial guesting. You can't do one or two and think you're done with podcasting; it has to be a sustained practice built over time. As you pitch and start to receive invites onto shows, it's important to carry on pitching.

Be an octopus

Reaching out across to the far corners of the planet has never been easier. Imagine yourself like an octopus reaching out to anyone with an internet connection. Think of the different themes in your message and story as tentacles, finding the right people and telling them what they are waiting to hear. Somewhere there will be people who need to receive the message that you are able to impart.

You have identified the different themes and topics reflected in your story so that you can fit your narrative to the individual podcast's requirements. When you are researching podcasts to guest on, don't dismiss those that seem out of your reach. Open your mind and think about what else you have to offer from the length and breadth of your experience and the deeper layers of your story.

Networking

Talk to people. Talk about podcasts. People listen to all kinds and will have favourites; they will love to tell you what they are enjoying at the moment. If you tell people that you are trying to get on podcasts, they will offer suggestions. There is nothing like word of mouth and a personal recommendation. Reach out on Clubhouse or Facebook groups that specialise in your area of expertise and ask if anyone has a podcast and is looking for guests. New podcast hosts run out of mates to interview pretty quickly and will be delighted if you send them an email saying you have listened to their show (do listen to their show) and would love to appear on it.

Create a strategy

Create an ongoing strategy. I recommend aiming to pitch to three podcasts a week. That may not seem much, but remember you have to listen to at least three episodes of each, analyse their DNA, find the contact address and tailor your pitch. This all takes time. Little and often is best, so that you don't get overwhelmed. Decide on a day and time in the week that you can set aside for podcast research and pitching. A systematic approach is sustainable and feels effortless, which means you'll keep at it.

EXAMPLE

With my podcast guesting agency clients, I have a system in place that you can replicate if you are going DIY.

- In our first session, they tell me their full back story.
- In our second session, we work out all their themes and topics.
- I then set up a spreadsheet. One tab is their themes and topics, the next is a list that I draw up of possible podcasts under different categories, with similar

reach. The headings on this tab include: podcast, podcast host, category, subject matter, reach, socials, contact, date submitted and status.

- My task is to listen to three episodes of three podcasts per week and submit to the client with curated pitches.

You should create your own system and strategy to suit your workload and lifestyle. Don't overwhelm yourself but keep it up with little and often over time.

Learnings

Get one podcast under your belt to see if it's your kind of thing and you want to use it as a marketing technique. If it is, you can now start to build a podcast guesting marketing strategy. Reach out across the globe like an octopus; you have several tentacles (themes and topics) that mean you can guest on podcasts across different categories and subject matters. Network widely but build relationships gradually and make sure people know that you are interested in podcast guesting. You should now be able to put a guesting system and strategy in place to help you move forward. Take the long view and keep pitching, regardless of your failures or successes.

ACTION STEPS

- Get one podcast under your belt.
- Research podcasts far and wide, go beyond your comfort zone.

- Think about how your story, themes and topics can be applied across various categories and subject matters.
- If you want to pursue podcast guesting as a marketing strategy, get a system in place.
- Work through your list of matched podcasts (mission, DNA and reach) and ideally submit to three per week.

Your worth

You might be worrying, who are you to be voicing your truth across the airwaves? But who are you not to? When you know your truth and your core values, you are better able to override that inner critic, build confidence and have courage in your convictions.

Speak your truth

Dare to share your truth. Not what others expect or want you to say. Not what you have been conditioned to say. Not what is polite to say. Dare to speak about yourself in a way that reflects the truth of who you are, what you do, what you believe, the path you're following, being your best self. This is you uncovered, open, standing up for the part of you that is unsure whether it is OK to speak your truth. It is OK.

Podcasts aren't just for marketing your wares, they are for helping to make the world a better place through your truth.

What is your truth? Your truth is reflected in your core values. These values are like your DNA. Knowing your values ensures you won't go on podcasts that don't sit right with you. They will inform the way you share your story with the world. For example, if you value equality, you won't go on a show that hasn't shown itself to be fully diverse and inclusive.

Spend time getting to know your values so that the podcasts you appear on reflect these. Start with ten core values, then narrow these down to five, then three. From these three you can create a mission statement that will guide you on your podcasting journey (and through life).

Confidence and self-sabotage

Yes, you will have knockbacks. Yes, your pitch will be ignored. Yes, you will be rejected. But when you feel strongly about your truth, your values, your story, your book, your business, your campaign, you will shake off these setbacks. Set your values against that sneaky, self-sabotaging voice that seeks to protect you from rejection and failure by preventing you from doing anything. But that's not where life happens, so when you hear that voice, write down what it has to say and then counter it with the opposing argument. Reassure the voice that you are prepared to take the risk of failure, for a chance of success.

The reason I recommend you use a system is to get past the fear of podcast guesting. Every step of the way, there will be something that could overwhelm you or knock your confidence. With a system and a strategy, and armed with your truth and core values, step by step you can build your confidence and fight the saboteur. Doing anything for the first time is hard. You may be confident in other areas of your life but here you are a newbie and it doesn't feel good. Everything feels like it's taking too long and you worry that it's a waste of time, that you will never be good at this whole podcast thing. But as with anything, practice makes perfect but perfection can be a hindrance so go for good enough, one pitch at a time, and you will become a master podcasting guest.

Have courage in your convictions

You know why it's important for you to get on podcasts to share your story. You know why you want to reach more people. You know that you're coming from a place of integrity and authenticity. You know there are people out there who need to hear what you have to say. You know that by doing this you will be helping to make the world a better place. Have courage in your convictions. Follow the steps, take the knockbacks and celebrate every inch of progress you make. Keeping your knowledge to yourself helps no one; sharing it helps many.

EXAMPLE

I asked Pam Millington to come on the BNG podcast. At first she was reluctant, shy, wondering what she had to say that would be of any interest to others. But her husband persuaded her. It was in the summer when the Black Lives Matter movement came to the fore. She could be another voice in the strengthening chorus. The world needed to pull up its bootstraps and get more inclusive and diverse, and podcasts were no exception. Hosts have the opportunity to share the space with people across the full spectrum of ethnicity, background, gender and sexuality, and potential guests needed to take up this space, speak up and speak out.

Pam came on and shared her experience of being the only black girl at school in an ex-pat area of Zambia and then, after marrying a Brit, moving to a very white village in rural Wiltshire. Being black seemingly raised no issues until her boys experienced racism at school, and Pam had to teach them to know their truth, to be proud of who they were and the skin they were in, to say their name, to embrace their mixed heritage and to let that be their backbone. When her boys flew the nest, she and her husband decided to return to Zambia to build a home on a plot of land and create a fishing camp to help boost tourism and the local economy. When I asked her how she defined courage she said it was the ability to see things through.

Pam had felt shy about her story, until she told her tale on the podcast. Then, when she listened to herself, she realised how many lessons there were in her journey for others to gain strength from.[19]

How many lessons are there in your story that will help others on their path?

Learnings

In this lesson, you have learned that knowing your worth, your truth and your core values helps you to build confidence over time and that with courage in your convictions you can overcome the self-sabotaging voice in your head. Knowing what truly matters to you and being prepared to speak your truth will enable to you to focus on pitching the podcasts that are right for you, with an audience ready to hear what you have to say. Be bold with who you are and what you stand for. Let your message be loud and clear. Have your mission at the forefront of your marketing strategy. You won't come across as salesy – you will appear as a force to be reckoned with, a powerhouse of integrity, a fountain of knowledge.

Speak your truth and live your values. Use the platform of podcasts to lead the way for others to do the same.

---

19 L Hamilton, 'Returning to Zambia to build a dream life in the African bush, with Pam Millington', Brave New Girl (2021), https://podcasts.apple.com/in/podcast/returning-to-zambia-to-build-dream-life-in-african/id1462548683?i=1000498177749

ACTION STEPS

- What is your truth? Write a stream of consciousness for ten minutes to explore this.
- Do the values exercise: narrow down your top ten to three.
- Write a mission statement based on your three core values.
- Write down your self-sabotaging messages and then the voice of reason.
- Find a podcast that sits uncomfortably with your values, and then one that sits well.

Summary

You have got yourself all the way to the point of pitching to podcasters, spreading your net and valuing what you have to offer. While you wait for replies, rinse and repeat. Read through the summary below and make sure that you are covering every aspect. If there are areas of weakness, work on those.

1. What podcasters want

You know how to find out what a podcast host wants for and from their show; to check that your story aligns with its DNA and that what you have to say is what the listeners want to hear. You do this by doing your homework on the show to understand its format, type of questioning and who the other guests have been.

You have worked out who their listeners are likely to be. You have researched the reach of the show and know that it roughly matches yours, although you can punch above your weight if you have good reason, and also approach a lesser followed show if you can see that it has high engagement.

2. Researching podcasts

You have a list of themes and topics to cover. You know how to search categories that cover your areas of interest. You know how to look for subcategories and home in on the podcasts that match your criteria, reach and mission. Now you're focused on the right podcasts, you know how to listen for their key elements: the types of questions, the format, their typical guests, the aims and objectives of the show. Once you feel confident you are the kind of guest the podcast host is after, you know how to search for their contact details and how you need to submit your proposal (a website form, social media or by email). You've written your biography and have a photograph ready for pitching.

3. How to pitch

You have learned how to prepare, how not to procrastinate and how to overcome a self-sabotaging inner voice. You've learned what to pitch and how to show the podcast host that you what you have to offer fits with the ethos of their show. You've learned how to create a system to store data on your contacts with podcast hosts so that you have an overview of who you have pitched to and what the outcome was. You know that you won't always hear back and may get rejections but you understand that that is part of the process and you need to persevere.

4. Spreading your net

If you decide after doing one podcast that you want to use podcast guesting as marketing strategy, create a system. With remote recording you can appear on any podcast anywhere in the world; reach out across the globe like an octopus, you have many tentacles that will enable you to guest on podcasts across different categories and subject matters. Network widely and build relationships, always letting people know that you are interested in podcast guesting. Keep moving forward and keep pitching, no matter the failures and successes, this is as ongoing strategy not a one-off activity.

5. Your worth

You have learned that knowing your worth, truth and core values helps you to build confidence over time and gives you courage in your convictions. This confidence and courage will enable you to overcome self-sabotage and doubt. When you know what truly matters to you and you are prepared to speak out on what this is, you can focus on pitching to the podcasts that are most aligned with your truth. The more you sit with your truth, the clearer it will become which podcasts to bypass and which to appeal to. The more you know about *why* you want to appear on particular podcasts, the stronger your pitch will be. Be bold about who you are and what you stand for. Let your message ring out loud and clear. Put your mission at the forefront of your marketing strategy.

Overview

You will be rejected, but by knowing your truth and your core values, countering your inner saboteur and growing your confidence through step by step progression, you will gain the courage in your convictions that will keep you moving forward over the long term. Pitch to a few podcasts every week, little and often. Be consistent. Have a system and a strategy. Rinse and repeat but remember to tailor your pitch and your email. Over time, your audience and reach will grow, opening up even more podcast opportunities for you.

FOUR

Getting The Gig

Between hearing that you have landed a podcast guest gig and appearing on the show, you have an opportunity to prepare and tailor your story. The better you know the show, the more targeted you can be and the more likely it is that listeners will engage with you.

After working through this chapter, you will feel fully prepared and ready to maximise your exposure to a whole new audience. We will cover the basic tasks you need to tick off in preparation for any podcast appearance:

- Do the admin

- Listen to the show

- Think about the questions

- Gift the listeners

- Technical rehearsal

Knowing a show's DNA, doing the necessary paper-work and checking the tech will make you a pro at using podcast guesting as a focused marketing strategy. Put in the preparation now and your performance will shine.

Do the admin

Even if you hate admin, your podcast host will love you if you are prepared; promptly send back their forms and/or any requested information, and show up on time. In this section, you will learn how to get yourself organised, schedule your time, understand release forms and make life easier for the podcaster.

Schedule the date and time

Expect some to-ing and fro-ing on this. The podcast hosts may have a set day and time that they record, or they may be happy to accommodate your schedule. Either way, when you set a date be sure that you are committed to it. It takes a lot of preparation on the part of the host to have you on the show so don't ask to move the date unless you have no choice.

As the time approaches, you might get nervous and think that you 'don't really need to be doing this pod-casting malarky'. Maybe something paid comes along and you're seduced into thinking you should do that over the podcast. Pull yourself up on this. Imagine your crowd listening to you, understanding your message, being hooked by your backstory enough to go buy your book, search for your website, sign up to your membership group, or support your campaign. There is everything to gain by committing to your date with a podcast host.

Understanding release forms

Release forms ensure that the podcast host can use the material you supply for and in your interviews across all forms of media, in all countries, for an indefinite period of time. Read the release forms, they are pretty routine across all podcasts. The legalese can seem over the top, but it is what is. Sign the form and return it to the host before the show – this might seem tedious but will only take five minutes of your time. Some pod-casters don't use these forms, but that's on them – they should really. You won't be given a chance to hear the edited interview before it airs so make sure you don't say anything that you don't want broadcast to the world. If you do say something by mistake, bring it up at the time of recording and ask the podcast host to repeat the question so you can give the reply that you want to go out on the airwaves. As a guest, you should not expect to have the right to request later edits – the majority of podcast hosts will not give you that option.

Provide your assets

The easier you can make the podcast host's life, the bet-ter. If you followed the earlier steps, when it comes to organising a guest appearance you will have already sent the host your biography as a Word document so that they can lift your details from there, alongside a high-resolution professional profile photograph. Check that they still have these; if they have been lost in podcasting administration, send them again.

Read the podcast episode show notes from other guests' episodes. Can you help the host by writing yours in their style? If you can, do. It's a time saver for the host, but from your perspective it means you get to summarise your life and work and can control how that comes across. They may not use it but at least you know they have accurate information and an overview of what you are about.

Provide the handles for all your socials and let the host know what hashtags you're using or would best suit whatever it is that you're promoting. If you have a link to your product or landing page, be sure to provide that too.

Now the host has what they need to be able to present you and your story correctly and ensure that the audience will be able to find and follow you after the show.

Check your landing page

Wherever you want people to find you, or whatever it is you want them to do – sign up for a freebie, buy your book, donate to your charity – make sure the link that you give to the podcast host is working. Check and double check.

While we are thinking about where you are directing the podcast audience, let's also consider what you want to get out of this precious opportunity. This is your chance to capture a whole new audience. The thing that should always be top priority is getting their email addresses. However you get them to sign up, use your podcast appearance to help grow your subscribers and mailing list.

Follow your podcast host

Any relationship needs to be nurtured. Before your interview, make sure you are following your host and the podcast across all platforms. Acknowledge and appreciate their output. Like their posts. Don't stalk or gush, just begin to build the relationship. Find where they are most engaged with their audience. Maybe your preferred port of call is Instagram but if your podcast host (and their audience) are mostly on Facebook then you need to be engaging with them there.

This is not some sycophantic love-in; it is about understanding the character of the host and what inspires their audience. What posts do their followers respond to most? What kind of comments do they leave? What need of the audience is being met by this person and/or show? If the host has an engaged feed, it should be easy to get a sense of the tone. When you leave a comment, their audience will read it so make sure it fits the vibe.

EXAMPLE

When we guested Emily Syphas of Sober and Social on the After Hours podcast, we scheduled in the time and they sent a standard release form for Emily to sign, as well as their outline questions and what Emily should expect during the interview. They also sent us, ahead of time, the links, handles and hashtags that we and Emily should use in sharing the episode when it came out. We followed and started commenting on their socials in the lead-up to the interview.

The episode was recorded face to face and was also being filmed, so Emily had to think about her hair, make-up and outfit. They took photos after the shoot which they turned into an illustration with their logo as their shareable asset. The whole process went smoothly because they had a good system in place. Not all podcasts are this organised, but when they are, you will be well prepared. Even if the podcast host doesn't seem to be as organised as this, you can be.[20]

Learnings

You have learned that admin is an unglamorous but essential element of podcast guesting. You need to set and commit to a recording date, remembering the impact you are going to make on the listeners to steady your nerves and stop you from bailing out last minute. Doing the legal legwork protects both you and the host and knowing that you can't expect editorial control means you will be careful about what you do and don't talk about on air. Getting your assets to your host with a

20 Astrid and Miyu, 'Social sobriety with Emily Syphas', After Hours S2 EP3, (2019), https://podcasts.apple.com/gb/podcast/after-hours-s2-ep3-social-sobriety-with-emily-syphas/id1479054355?i=1000468758454

well-written and concise biography will ensure that the show notes provide the listeners with the information you want them to know and encourage them to listen to your episode. You know to make sure your landing page and other links are up to date and working. This is your opportunity to bring the podcast listeners into your fold, don't waste it. Now you also understand the importance of engaging fully with your podcast host across all their social platforms to build a relationship with them in advance of your interview.

ACTION STEPS

- Get yourself a good diary system.
- Read, understand and sign the host's release form.
- Have your assets ready and decide what hashtags and handles you want the host to use.
- Check your landing page and any other links you want the listener to follow.
- Engage with the podcast hosts that you're guesting with on all socials.

Listen to the show

You might not have time to listen to a whole series of the podcast you're guesting on, but you do need to have a good handle on what it's about so try to listen as much as possible. You can do this while you're doing boring mundane jobs at home, killing two birds with one stone.

In this section you will learn how to 'actively' listen to the podcast you are due to appear on. Active listening is learning. Learning is knowledge. And knowledge is what you need when you are sat in the hot seat.

Active listening

When we listen actively we listen to obtain information, to understand, for enjoyment and to learn. Normally, when you listen to a podcast you are probably mainly listening for enjoyment, but you may also, depending on the podcast, be listening to learn. In this case, when you have a gig coming up and are listening to the podcast episodes, you are listening to learn, understand and obtain information. You need to know the format, the style and the types of questions. Is it conversational? Does it have a quick-fire round? Is it a host and one guest, or two hosts, or multiple guests? Is it a teaching podcast? Is it witty, or wise? Pay attention and focus on what the host in particular is saying. Even better, take notes.

What is the host trying to give to their listeners by asking the guests the types of questions they do? What direction are they taking the guest in? If the host themselves is a good listener they will have set questions that they intended to ask but will also be picking up on and responding to what the guest is saying. That's often when the conversation gets interesting. It is a process of exploration, not simply a Q & A. When the host trusts themselves to curate the conversation while staying in tune with their guest, the exchange feels alive, responsive, quick witted and exciting.

The host

When you are actively listening to understand the show, you need to also get a feel for how well the host listens. Will you be riffing off each other, or are the questions fairly set in stone? Try to understand what the host is searching for, what they want to extract for their listeners? What can you give them that will fit their style?

The host will hopefully be a good listener, giving the guest space to tell their story, get their message across and enlighten the listeners with their experience, expertise and lessons learned. However, if the host has less helpful listening skills, it is good to know this ahead of time. Do they tend to interrupt the guest with their own anecdotes? Do they fail to listen at all and plough on with pre-determined questions?

Knowing the listening style of the host will mean you won't be derailed if they interrupt you, seem distracted or respond with their own contribution. You can't change their listening style but being prepared will allow you to adapt to it and get your story back on track when you can.

The listener

When you're listening to the podcast, you should also try to do so from the perspective of the podcast listener. Sometimes, when the host and guest get caught up in their enjoyment of their conversation, they forget the listeners. The audience feels that; they feel disconnected, leading to a lack of rapport with host and guest and less engagement with the episode. They feel on the outside, not in with the 'cool gang'.

When you're preparing to be the guest, be mindful of the audience. You will still be focused on and listening to the host, but remember you are addressing the listeners. When you are listening, work out what makes you feel engaged with and part of the episode and what makes you feel excluded.

Listen to learn

Listening is the key to communication and human relationships. When we listen to learn, we tune in so attentively that we are able to pick up every underlying message and appreciate the subtleties of the connection between the host and guest. Learn how to be a great guest by listening out for the guests that inspire you. What can you learn from their responses, the way they convey their message and tell their stories, the generosity with which they share their lives with the audience?

Real listening takes practice. Taking notes will help you remain tuned in. Listen not just to the words but to the emotions beneath them. Taking this time to listen to the podcast series with a willingness to learn what works and what is less effective, will make you a better guest.

EXAMPLE

When Annabelle Mu'azu, founder of lingerie brand IHUOMA, guested on BNG, it was her first time on a podcast. On listening, you'd think she was a confident person, that guesting on a podcast wouldn't faze her. But when you hear her talk about why she designs lingerie and the message she is trying to send – when she worked in the corporate world she wore lingerie as armour, as her secret weapon, her confidence charger – you realise that within the impressive entrepreneur are the same doubts and fears the rest of us have.

Annabelle used lingerie to empower herself, which is why she created a brand to empower other women. The concept of luxury lingerie is transformed from something for rich women into something more accessible, no longer a frivolous purchase, but a message to yourself that you are worth it.[21]

By listening deeply to this episode we hear so much more than the story of a brand. We hear the truth of the founder and may learn something about ourselves.

---

21 L Hamilton, 'Celebrating your sensuality with lingerie designer Annabelle Mu'Azu', Brave New Girl (2020), https://podcasts.apple.com/in/podcast/celebrating-your-sensuality-lingerie-designer-annabelle/id1462548683?i=1000503291115

Learnings

Active listening takes us deeper into people's stories. We learn more, we understand more, we enjoy more, we engage more. When you listen to a podcast you can pick up on the way in which a host listens and responds to their guest and can prepare yourself to be interrupted, or to be listened to intently. You will know whether the host will stick to their set questions no matter what you say, or whether they will adapt and respond to you in a more natural conversation.

Now you also have listened to the podcast from the perspective of the audience. You know what alienates you and what draws you in and intrigues you. When you are a guest on that podcast you will be better able to engage the listeners because you understand what makes their ears prick up and or what makes them tune out. By understanding how guests can be most enlightening, you can dare to share. You know that effective communication is not one sided, but requires both listening and talking.

ACTION STEPS

- Actively listen to the podcast you are to appear on to know format, style and types of questions.
- Listen to understand whether the host is a good listener and how they respond to their guests.

- Identify any listening habits to watch out for from the host, such as interruption.
- As a member of the audience, how do the host and guest make you feel? Are they aware of you as the audience? Do they make you feel included?
- Listen to the guest to learn what works well or not so well in podcast storytelling. Take on the positive traits in your approach.

Consider the questions

You might be worried about what questions the host will ask you. Remember, they aren't trying to catch you out; their questions should be a springboard for you to tell your story. In this section, we'll talk about how to prepare for answering the podcaster's questions. If they have sent you some in advance, great, you can mull over how you might respond. If they haven't, working through this section will ensure you know how to respond.

Pre-set versus unknown questions

In the best case scenario, the host sends you an outline of the questions they are going to ask, so you can prepare more precisely in the areas they want you to talk about. If they do give you a heads up, it is more likely that they will give you general pointers rather than specific questions. This still helps you to prepare broad answers across a range of topics. It is unlikely that the host will stick exactly to their set of questions and that's good because it allows you to be more fluid in your answers. If you read verbatim from pre-prepared answers, it will sound wooden and unnatural. You can't do anything about it if a host is reading out their questions in this way, but you can at least know your material well enough to be confident in going with the flow yourself. Later in this section, you will learn how to prepare answers for pre-set and unknown questions.

If the host doesn't send you any questions or rough areas they intend to cover, there are still ways you can prepare. You will have to guess what they might ask you, so go back and listen to the format of the show. Over a few episodes, you should get a sense of what themes and types of questions the host returns to time and again. If a show is long-running it will have evolved and honed its message and format, so look to the most recent shows to mine for up-to-date information.

Types of questions

If a host is worth their salt, they will avoid closed questions. These invite yes-or-no answers and lead to nowhere. Even the best of hosts might slip in the odd closed question by mistake, so be prepared and be generous enough to expand even when they haven't given you much room to do so. By contrast, open questions ask who, why, when, what, where, how. Think about these ahead of time. They are useful in bringing up different aspects of your story. Another approach is for a host to give you choices or options in their questions; they probably know which way you will go but it makes things more interesting for the listener. Then there is the slightly provocative, maybe a little antagonistic question that edges you out of your comfort zone. This is usually used in an investigative line of questioning, but you never know, a podcast host might try to push you in this way. Again, by studying the podcast series you'll know what kinds of questions the host asks and whether they ever veer toward this style.

The art of questioning is to elicit answers in such a way that a sense of story is created, with a beginning, a middle and an end, with highs and lows, challenges and triumphs, and a glimpse of the future. The listeners should feel they are being taken along for the ride, and you as the guest should be part of the natural to-ing and fro-ing. The best way to feel able to surrender to this process is to do as much preparation as possible.

You have control over how you prepare your answers. The world is mysterious, ambiguous and equivocal and the reason listeners are intrigued by what you have to say is that they believe there will be something in your story that gives them answers. The host is the mouthpiece for an audience who want to understand the mysteries of the world and their place within it, so think of interesting anecdotes, perspectives and interpretations to have in your arsenal of answers.

Preparing possible answers

If the host has sent the questions in advance, you can make notes on your answers. If they don't, listen to questions in previous episodes and think about how you would answer them. Write out a timeline of your potted history (you should already have this from the exercises in the story chapter) and as you think of particular anecdotes and relevant topics around the podcast themes, jot them down along the timeline. Do this over the week before the interview, not in the five minutes before. Stories will pop into your mind when you are in the shower, at the gym or when your mind is idly wandering. Ask yourself questions and let your thoughts drift around possible replies. Then, drill deeper with potential follow-up questions. Why did that happen? What was really going on? How could you have done that differently? Did that terrible event throw some light on what you should do next? What lessons did you learn? At what point did you decide to do things differently? Jog your memory with inquiring questions. Read through your notes the day before the interview, then trust in the process and let the host be your guide.

EXAMPLE

When Annabelle Mu'azu was coming on the podcast (remember it was her first time), I sent her some rough questions around our theme. I kept it simple, because from what I read in her biography, her story was quite complicated and multi-layered. I gave her the tent pegs on which she could expand:

Pandemic: You launched a new lingerie brand IHUOMA in the middle of a global pandemic

Past: Cocoa Arts, Beautifully Undressed etc

Passion: Empowering women

Pain points: What have been the biggest challenges and what have you learned about yourself through these experiences?

Purpose: Creating lingerie for black women

Peaks: What have been the highlights?

Possibilities: From where you are right now, what is your vision for your future?

This rough guide with some prompts was enough for her to know what she needed to think about before we talked. Look through the work you have done on your story, your themes and topics and your potted history timeline – you will have plenty of material to work with. Add to that your understanding of the specific areas of questioning that will be brought up in the podcast you are about to appear on, and you will be good to go.

Learnings

You have learned how to prepare for all eventualities and can make notes on possible answers, whether the host sends you the topics beforehand or you have to guess the kinds of questions they will ask. You know that you can gain a lot of insight into the style of questioning they will pursue by listening to and analysing previous episodes. By making notes you will jog your memory and have some concrete responses to hand. You will also have your timeline, potted history and the side stories and anecdotes that fit along the way. You have asked yourself layered questions so that you can provide in-depth answers and have considered the kinds of information that the listeners might find enlightening. You know that once you have done your preparations, with your self-knowledge at your fingertips, you can trust the host to guide you through the interview.

ACTION STEPS

- Prepare answers to any questions or topics sent in advance.

- Make notes on the types of questions your host asks across other episodes so you can guess what might come up.

- Question yourself using the four types of questions identified in this section and try to expand on your answers as much as possible.

- Think about the kinds of lessons the podcast listeners want to learn and think about how you can offer this to them.

- Carry a notebook around with you in your preparation week so you can easily make a note of any stories that you remember.

Gift your listeners

You want to think about what it is that the podcast listeners need. When you shift your perspective to see the listener as the hero on a journey and yourself as a guide, it will be clear what you need to give them. Work out exactly what you want your listeners to take away from your interview. From earlier sections, you'll already have a landing page ready, or a link, a freebie or sign-up page. But more importantly, you'll be speaking to them as a guide on their journey. If you get it right, this will be the beginning of a long and happy relationship.

The most important thing you can do in your preparation is to understand what the podcast you are guesting on is offering its listeners. You should be able to find it in their show notes if they have taken the time to clearly identify and communicate this. For example, on Brave New Girl, we talk about different ways people can find courage to get through the chaotic business of life and work. Read through the show notes of several podcasts and see if you can identify what it is that they are offering their listeners.

The listener is the hero, you are the guide

But wait, you thought you were the hero, going on the podcast to talk about your story, your journey? You are, but to what end? You are going on podcasts to sell or raise awareness of something, of course, but the listeners aren't going to buy from or engage with you further unless you are solving a problem for them. According to Donald Miller in his book *Building a StoryBrand*,[22] unless you are helping people to survive, thrive, find love or benefit them in some other way in their own hero's journey, they will move on to someone who does.

How can you make the listener your focus while telling your story? You emphasise the lessons you have learned from your experiences. You share your dark night of the soul but then you explain to them how you came out into the light in the end. You share your triumphs but you also reveal the daily practice and hard work it took to master your sport, your business, your art. You tell them how you found your sense of purpose, and where you believe it will take you. What does all this mean in the grand scheme of things?

You are the guide on the listener's journey. When you share your story generously and with gentle guidance in mind, the listener will feel that they have found you just when they needed to hear what you have to say. What problems are you solving for the listener? What message can you glean from your story that might help the audience? What insights can you share, based

---

22   D Miller, *Building a StoryBrand: Clarify your message so customers will listen* (HarperCollins Leadership, 2017)

on the life you have lived thus far? What advice can you impart, drawing from your expertise?

When the listener hears your tale, they should be able to take it with them as guidance on the next part of their journey. What signposts, tools and lessons can you gift them?

In your preparation, think about the aspects of your story that may have universal meaning. Were you once an outsider but found a way to use that to your advantage? For example, watching the world from the outside and using your observations to improve your novel writing. Being an outsider can be lonely. Many people can relate to that feeling. Turning this position into that of an observer flips that negative feeling on its head and draws something positive. With this new perspective, someone might feel that they are on a mission; that they have been gifted with the ability to stand back, at the edge, unnoticed and able to observe elements of life that are missed by those in the thick of the throng. Your listener might take that knowledge and change their mindset.

Understand your role as guide and be clear about the gifts you come bearing. The listener will carry these gifts with them long after they have listened to the podcast. They may adjust their own story as a result. It may give them the confidence to move forward in a way they were hesitant to do before. Your words will land in some way, it is up to you to ensure you have given the best guidance you can. Beyond the podcast episode, you can build on your new relationship and invite the audience to engage with you further by providing a more tangible gift that they can access on your website. In exchange for their much-coveted email address, you can offer them a free gift following up on elements from your story. This can be anything, but make sure it's related to whatever it is you're promoting; this leads to a more engaged customer or client. Make sure you prepare the free gift in advance of your interview and give the information to the host ahead of time, in case they record links before the show.

EXAMPLE

I recently interviewed holistic medical consultant Dr Vidhi Pandya Patel for the opening episode of a new season of BNG. The listener was coming into the New Year full of festive cheer, alcohol and rich foods and perhaps regretting their over-indulgence. It's a lethargic and bloated start to the year, tinged slightly with regret and plastered with promises to do better. Vidhi, as a guide, does not reprimand but gently suggests simple, easy-to-action adjustments. Nothing arduous, and totally manageable. This was her gift to the listener. She talked about her work and the benefits she aims to give her clients, and about the people she has helped along the way. If, by the end of the podcast, the listener feels like they trust Vidhi and want to know more, they can visit the website and access further information. If they are still on board after that, they might follow up by making an appointment to see Vidhi, cementing their relationship.

Think of what you are gifting your listener as the start of what could become a long and rewarding relationship.[23]

Learnings

You have learned to put the listeners at the front of your mind, positioning them as the hero and using what you have to say to help them on their journey. When you adopt the role of guide you will shift how you tell your story. You will be mindful of drawing out the lessons you have learned from your experiences and the insights and expertise you can impart as a result of your own growth and evolution. You will give these as gifts to the listener, golden nuggets they can take with them as they fight their own battles. Then, once this relationship has been established, you will cement it further by giving them a reason to engage with you beyond the podcast. This will be an exchange of gifts; they give you their email or make a first purchase and you give them something that makes it worth their while.

23 L Hamilton, 'Getting your health on in 2021 with Dr Vidhi Patel', Brave New Girl (2021), https://podcasts.apple.com/in/podcast/getting-your-health-on-for-2021-with-dr-vidhi-patel/id1462548683?i=1000504466338

ACTION STEPS

- Work out what the podcast is offering its listeners.
- Shift your story to make the listener the hero.
- As the listeners' guide, think about what problem you are solving for them.
- Write out your five top tips for the listener.
- Set up a landing page for your gift exchange.

Technical rehearsal

Now we've covered the meat of the interview and what you hope to offer and achieve, it's time to get technical. Podcasts rely on a lot of technology, but what if you're a technophobe? What if you don't have access to a podcast studio? Recording a podcast is certainly not as straightforward as jumping on a Zoom meeting, but don't worry, it's not hard to do a good DIY job. If you are going into a studio, everything will be set up for you. If you're doing it from home, we're here to help.

A podcaster's worst nightmare is a guest with bad sound. In this section, I will talk you through how to ensure you have good (enough) sound and explain exactly how to prepare all the technical stuff so that you can conquer the airwaves, even if you are having to do so remotely.

Dampen the room

Don't get too hung up on trying to achieve perfection. Remote recording will never match the quality of a studio recording but there are some easy steps you can take to improve the sound that your host will thank you for. First, try and dampen the space you are going to be recording in. The smaller the space, the better – think under the stairs or in a broom cupboard. If you can't do that, try setting up in the corner of a room and barricade yourself in with chairs or screens and throw towels, rugs, blankets or duvets over the top. If you imagine the soundwaves moving away from you and banging into screens close by, they don't have much time to echo back at you. The farther they can travel before hitting a wall and bouncing back, the greater the echo. Visualising how soundwaves travel helps you understand why it is important to deaden the sound and how to achieve this. One thing to consider when choosing your recording location is whether it's in a good WiFi spot. If it's weak, is there somewhere suitable where the signal is better?

Use a headset

When you're on Zoom calls, you probably don't bother with all the paraphernalia of remote recording. You click on the link and off you go – no mic, no headphones, just you and your computer. But if you're going to do podcast guesting as a regular part of your marketing strategy, you need to take it seriously and be prepared. The podcast hosting platform will require that you wear headphones. These don't have to be state of the art, they can be cheap plug-in earphones, but you need to have something. Check in advance that both your computer and the hosting platform can 'see' your headphones.

Browser alert

Some podcast recording platforms only work with specific browsers. The podcast host should tell you what browser works for them but I have known guests not to take notice and then wonder why they can't get onto the show. The host will be able to help you with some troubleshooting but it takes time to sort out a technical issue and you can end up feeling flustered and unprepared when you finally manage to get started with the interview. Find out beforehand which browser is supported by the recording platform and make sure you already have it downloaded, made a note of any technical requirement and have got everything sorted and tested ahead of time.

Going pro

You can absolutely wing it with ear pods and a laptop, but if podcast guesting is going to be a serious part of your marketing efforts, it helps to have the right gear. It's also encouraging for the podcast host. Any good host will have a listen to other podcasts you have been a guest on – they have your biography but there is nothing like hearing you talk to decide if you are right for their show. If the quality of your recording is poor then, no matter how good your story is, it could put them off – they don't want bad sound on their show. Even if they do ask you to join them on their podcast, it might put listeners off – the better quality your sound, the easier and more enjoyable it will be to listen to you. So if you want to go down the podcasting route, it would be wise to invest in a decent set of headphones and a professional mic.

Practice makes perfect

There is nothing like doing something repeatedly to get comfortable with it. Thinking about it is not the same. The Covid-19 pandemic forced people to get much more comfortable with talking to someone via a screen, but whether you have been on podcasts before or have been doing back-to-back Zoom calls throughout the pandemic, you still haven't been on this particular podcast, with its unique slant. Though you'll only record this podcast once, you can still practise – get your story notes, the themes you are going to cover, and the questions the host might ask, then set up your mic and headphones and practise talking out loud.

Overcome your nerves by testing your sound levels with a bit of chatter. Get comfortable with the sound of your voice. If it sounds squeaky with nerves, breathe with your belly, wiggle your tongue, pretend to chew on a giant piece of bubblegum. Now practise some of your answers. Remember to focus on the listener. Once you have done a technical rehearsal, learned to relax your voice, run through some possible answers and kept your mind on the listeners' needs, you will be good to go.

EXAMPLE

I have had guests who haven't been ready or prepared. Some have forgotten their headphones and found themselves running round the house looking for some, or worse, have had to rearrange the interview for a time when they have managed to borrow some equipment. Some guests have got the wrong time entirely, or forgotten to install the right browser so they couldn't log on to the recording platform. Or they didn't put the dog out. Or their phone wasn't on silent. You name it, a guest has done it. As a host, I have become used to troubleshooting the technical hitches that arise from a guest's ill-preparedness, but it is a stressful way to start an interview and you can easily avoid the issues by getting set up ahead of time.

Learnings

You're nearly there now. With all the hard work and preparation you have done thus far, you are going to shine on air. Just a final reminder: dampen the room you are going to record in, make sure you have your headset or headphones set up, install the correct browser for the platform you'll be using and test your mic if you have gone pro. Then practise using your whole setup. Remember to do all this in advance. There is nothing worse than realising you don't have everything set up correctly and keeping the host waiting while you sort yourself out. If you are ready ahead of time, there will be no nasty surprises and you can focus on your performance.

Boom. You're ready.

ACTION STEPS

- Dampen the room or space you are going to record in.
- Make sure you have your headset/headphones set up and they are recognised by your computer and the podcast recording platform.
- Install the correct browser for the platform the podcast will be recorded on.
- Test your mic, if you are using one.
- Practise with your whole setup.

Summary

Well done for completing this chapter. It's not the most fun part of the process, but by doing your technical preparation you free yourself up to enjoy the performance. Here's a summary of where you're at now:

Do the admin

You've filled in the release form if the host provided one. You've made sure the host has your biography and a good profile photo for them to use in the show notes and promote the episode. You've ensured your landing page is working and is geared toward taking the listener/customer further in their journey with you. You are now following and engaging with your podcast host across various social networks.

Listen to the show

You have listened to a few episodes of the show you'll be appearing on and you understand the host's style of questioning and listening, as well as the overall format of the show. You have listened from the perspective of the audience and know what makes you tune in or zone out. You have also actively listened to the guests to get a sense of when they are at their most enlightening and engaging. You've made a decision about how much you are going to share, so that in the flow of the conversation you don't get swept up in the enthusiasm of being on the show and forget your boundaries.

Consider the questions

The host has sent you some general questions and themes in advance and you've prepared some answers based on those. You've also identified the type of questions the host asks in the flow of the show, you know whether they're formulaic or flow from the last thing the guest has said. When you listened to previous episodes you made notes on the kinds of answers you would give to the general questions they commonly ask. You've made sure your answers have multiple layers in case the host decides to explore a topic in depth. You've drawn up a timeline so that you have a clear chronology of events and plenty of side stories along the way and have highlighted any areas you particularly want to talk about.

Gift the listeners

You have put the listeners front of mind. You know why they tune into the show and what they want to learn. You know what you can give them that will enhance their own experience. You're treating the listener as the hero navigating their journey, and you see yourself as the guide shining a light on their path. You've thought about what lessons you've learned from your challenges that they can use in their own battles and struggles. You've identified where your successes came through hard work, visualisation or luck. You are gifting your experiences to the listener hoping that they will be inspired and open up to you by following you, making a purchase, visiting your landing page and giving you their email address. You offer a free gift so that the listeners want to be in your gang.

Technical rehearsal

Even if you are well practised in recording, it is always worthwhile doing a quick technical run through. You never know when gremlins will sneak into the works. Remember to dampen the room where possible to deaden any echoes. Make sure your headset or headphones and mic, if you're using one, are set up. Be sure you have the correct browser on your computer for the recording platform – for example, at the time of writing, Squadcast is not supported by Safari. Do all this in advance of the interview, not two minutes before, in case there is a technical hiccup. Just before the interview, make sure the washing machine isn't turned on, any pets are happy and kids are occupied. Turn off the fan, close the windows and tell everyone in your household that you won't be available for the next hour.

If preparation is the key, you are now ready to open the door and walk through for your grand entry. The stage is yours, go get 'em!

FIVE

Showtime

This is where the fun starts. All the work you have done up to now has given you wings to fly from podcast to podcast, gifting listeners with your story. Now you can share your message and offer your guidance on podcasts, stages, radio, YouTube or any other audio/video medium that gives a platform to people like you for the greater good. This chapter is about your actual performance – it's showtime.

Once you have worked through this chapter, you will be fully prepared for your performance. When you have done this inner work you won't be fazed by different requirements or setups, or the hiccups that will inevitably happen as you tour various podcasts. Over time, you will master your performance and fine tune it, adding nuance and evolution to your story. But for now, as a novice, you'll at least be ready to cut your teeth. In this chapter, we will cover:

- Recording preparation
- Voice/physical preparation
- Being a guiding light

- Getting in the flow

- Giving thanks

You are going to be an awesome guest. You will be fully prepared to give a great performance, be fully present, use your full voice, speak your truth and leave the listeners wanting more.

Recording preparation

In this section, you will learn how to show up to the mic, on time and ready to roll. You may have a last minute panic but you've done your preparations and you know everything is set up and working. Aside from technology, there are a few other things to consider and prepare.

Check your environment

It's a good idea to have a wipeboard by your computer with a checklist so that you can run through your checks like a pilot every time you record. The more podcasts you do, the more relaxed you will become – relaxed is good, but forgetful isn't, so get into the habit of running through your checks. Start by always giving yourself half an hour before the interview begins. Rushing in from another meeting is not a good way to get your head in the right place, so give yourself the time to get settled.

Check your environment. Are all noisy machines off? Is your phone on silent? Have you created a snug around your computer to dampen the sound? If you are being videoed, is your backdrop suitable? Are dogs, children, partners fully aware that you are going to be recording, and been suitably bribed, cajoled or persuaded to be quiet for an hour or so? Are the windows shut? Is that rattling radiator turned off?

When you've ticked off all your environment checks, your space is ready.

Check tech

The next items on your checklist will be tech related. We touched on this in the last chapter when you were preparing and practising, but it's even more important for the real deal. If you are using an external mic, check it's on, and working. Are your headphones plugged in? This is not a joke. I have known people to put on their headphones and wonder why there is no sound, only to discover the end of the wire is trailing along the carpet. Is the computer seeing your headphones? Check this in the settings. If you are signing into a recording platform like Squadcast, in the 'green room' it will ask you to check the headphones, mic and camera that you are using. In your previous rehearsal you will have established that you are in a good WiFi spot and are signing in on the right kind of device with the correct browser, so that's all you need to do before each recording session. Not too bad, right?

Check sound

Once you've signed into whatever platform you are recording on, you'll have a chance to double check the sound levels and make any adjustments you need to. If you are wearing plug-in earphones they can sometimes be a bit crackly if you move about or knock the wires, so try to sit still. Do this now before you start recording. If you are using a proper mic, check the levels. Don't be too close and watch out for popping.

Check video

Most people are pretty used to using video now, so this is just a quick reminder that visual impressions are important. It adds another layer to the audience's experience by making them both a viewer and a listener. When they are simply a listener their brain will focus completely on what you are saying; when video is added to the mix they will have the distractions of looking at the spines of the books behind you, or admiring the artwork on the wall, or wondering when you last had your roots done. Essentially, the more visual stimuli they have, the harder it will be for them to listen intently and deeply to your message, story, advice or experience. Make it easier for them and keep your background and appearance simple and free of visual distraction. If you have a separate plug-in camera from the built-in one, make sure it is connected and recognised by the recording platform. Check the lighting and how you look on screen, then consciously relax your body and face – and remember to smile.

By taking this half hour to run final checks, you will be unflustered and methodical. In the last five minutes, the last check to do is to check in with yourself. Having got this far through the book, you know that you are as prepared as you can be. You have your story, topics and themes both in your mind and to hand. You understand the needs of the listeners of the podcast you are about to appear on and what you hope to enlighten them with to feed their hearts, minds and souls. Now you have a few minutes to breathe and thank yourself for all that work you have done thus far. Trust that you know everything you need to and that that you have done everything you can. If anything goes wrong during the interview, or tech gremlins rock up unexpectedly, you can be reassured that you have done your checks and it couldn't have been avoided. Take one more slow belly breath, sit or stand tall, shoulders back and put a prayer in to the tech gods.

EXAMPLE

You get people trying to join the recording platform, while running round the house attempting to get a WiFi signal, looking for headphones, trying to shut the dog up, answer the front door to the postman and searching for their notes. Those who aren't prepared and haven't given themselves the time to set up and do their checks are inevitably those that are running against the clock, getting to the interview in the nick of time and feeling flustered. When problems crop up, which they do, they then take up the podcaster's time trying to sort out whatever issue has occurred. Most hosts are pretty understanding about tech problems, but this interferes with their own state of preparedness. They will have got themselves into the zone ready to bring out the best in you, but instead of an easy segue into the interview, they are wrestling with getting things sorted out your end. Sometimes it can't be helped, but by doing your checks, you've given it your best shot. And the host will be grateful for that.

Learnings

In this section, you have learned the importance of preparedness. You've made your environment as recording-friendly as possible. You've got to grips with the technology and have created a checklist that covers your environment, tech, sound video and yourself. You know to give yourself half an hour to run through this checklist every time you record and that, no matter how many podcasts you end up doing, you should always carve out this time before you begin, to troubleshoot and get in the zone. You know the importance of arriving at the mic calm and collected and taking the time to breathe, release tension and get comfortable, in the perfect state to do the interview.

ACTION STEPS

- Check your environment is conducive to recording.
- Check that you understand what tech is required for each podcast recording.
- Check your sound levels and quality.
- Check that nothing that can be seen on the video is distracting.
- Check in with yourself to ensure you are calm, prepared and comfortable.

Voice preparation

Many people dislike the sound of their own voice on a recording. Maybe you think your accent is hard to understand, your tone too high pitched, or you're too hesitant. There are some practical preparations you can do to strengthen your voice. No matter what your accent, if you are shy, if performance is not your bag, once you've worked through this section your voice is going to carry your message to the world.

Power pose

Just before the show, pump up your energy, puff out your chest and throw your arms outstretched into the air. Fill the space around you, run on the spot, do some tongue twisters out loud. Generally loosen up and liven up. There is a great yoga pose where you stand with your feet hip width apart, arms loose at your side and knees slightly softened. Slowly start to swing your body side to side, looking over each shoulder and letting your hands flow with your body as you swing. Start slow and then speed up. When you are at full speed, stop. Allow your arms to hang at your side and bring your awareness to the energy fizzing through your body, then let that energy calm until you feel still.

Sit up straight

Sit up straight in the chair where you are going to record. Don't hunch or you will constrict your voice. You can hear if someone is playing small, if their body language is closed with legs crossed, arms crossed and shoulders hunched. This kind of pose squashes your voice and your spirit. You will sound closed and dull, like everything is forced or you are reluctant to reveal something. By opening your body you will sound open-hearted and open-minded, showing yourself to be vulnerable.

Belly breath

Practise belly breathing beforehand so your body and mind are relaxed and your throat isn't tight. Your voice will sound full and lower pitched, which is easier to listen to and sounds more professional. As you sit tall in your chair, feel how your neck has elongated, with your chin tucked in slightly and the top of your head pulled up as if by a string. Roll your shoulders back and down. Place one hand on your belly and breathe in through your nostrils for three counts, filling your belly so that it pushes outwards, then breathe out through your nostrils for seven counts. You should feel your belly flatten again with your hand. Take three or four rounds of deep belly breaths like this; it will calm your nerves and settle your mind.

Chew the cud

This is a weird one, but chewing on a bit of apple before recording will prevent that clacking sound people can make. You are right in people's ears and they don't want to hear the sound of saliva and teeth. Munching on a piece of fruit moistens the mouth. Chew it like a cow chews the cud, with big, exaggerated circles of your jaw, one way and then the other. When all the muscles of your face are nicely loosened up, get your tongue wagging this way and that. Then take another deep belly breath in and release out with a series of 'la, la, las'. Same again with 'loo, loo, loos'. Then 'lah, lah, lah' and 'lee, lee, lee'. These mouth, throat and voice gymnastics get you ready for producing a strong, even sound when you speak. I know it feels silly, but it's worth it.

Become aware

If you are thinking of a hundred things at once – what you have to do today, what your kids are up to, worrying about your bank balance, or the future of the planet – your attention won't be fully on the interviewer and you may lose your thread. You will know what it's like to have a conversation with someone who isn't quite 'with you', they seem distracted and disengaged and you can hear it in their voice. The brain can't do two things properly at the same time, so put aside the rest of your day, the rest of your life, your troubles and strife, and bring your awareness to the mic. Have your notes to hand, take another deep breath and focus on the host. Be prepared for when a stray thought comes to mind and bring your attention back to the questions they ask you. Turn everything else off and fix your awareness on the present; here, now, with the host – your focus will translate in the tone of your voice.

EXAMPLE

My guests have all been great and put aside the time to give the podcast their full attention. Penny Power OBE is a particularly good example because she is a natural at making you feel that, in this moment, you are the most important person in her world. She has mastered the art of being fully present and appreciative of the space you are giving her with the podcast. She listens intently to the questions and is thoughtful with her answers. You feel like she is weighing up the full depth of the conversation and honouring it by giving considered answers. She speaks clearly and deliberately, because she is fully present, making her a pleasure to listen to. I'd urge you to listen to any podcast she is on.[24]

---

24 L Hamilton, 'Business is Personal with Penny Power OBE', Brave New Girl (2021), https://podcasts.apple.com/in/podcast/business-is-personal-with-penny-power-obe/id1462548683?i=1000518888793

Learnings

You have learned to give energy to your body by pumping yourself up with a power pose. You know to sit straight while recording so you don't constrict your voice. You know how to breathe deeply in a way that calms your nervous system. You can give your mouth and tongue a good work out and stretch to loosen and relax your voice. Finally, you know the importance of focusing on the task at hand by blocking out all other thoughts and keeping your awareness on the present moment so that you sound engaged and confident.

ACTION STEPS

- Practise your power pose.
- Learn how to sit straight and recognise how it feels.
- Practise belly breathing.
- Do your mouth exercises.
- Practise bringing and keeping your awareness on the present moment.

Guiding light

You are the guide, and your story shines a light on the experiences of the listeners. When you are vulnerable and open and come to the mic in a thoughtful and considerate state of mind, listeners will learn more from who you are and how you come across than they will from the details of what you do.

The podcast listener is on their own journey. They have battles they are fighting, challenges they are trying to overcome, doubts about whether they are doing the right thing, dreams of winning, fear of failing, pride getting in their way, various balls they're trying to keep in the air. Maybe they're feeling anger at having been let down, shame that they've let themselves down, guilt if they've hurt people in pursuit of their passion and purpose, grief at losing people along the way. The listener is hoping you will offer them something that gives them the courage not to give up, the inspiration to aim higher, or faith that all will be well. They are giving you a portion of their time because they believe you will help them on their way.

From your perspective, the point of guesting on multiple podcasts is to build a tribe of people who will be drawn to whatever it is you have to offer. They can either listen to your episode, be entertained and walk away none the wiser, or you can use your story to help them find their way. When you act as a guide, the listener will be more actively engaged in what you have to say, recognising that it is grease to their wheel. As a storyteller, you are not there to blow your own trumpet but to be a foghorn for the listener that they can trust and follow.

Signal and serve

A good guide provides signals. What signal points in your story can shine a light for the listener? When you can bring out of your story moments of awareness, you can share these insights. Turn the 'I' into 'you'. For example, 'I learned to let go of the outcome, and just focused on what action I could take in any given moment' becomes, 'Let go of the outcome, just focus on what action you can take in any given moment.' When you turn lessons from your story into signal points for the listener, they will recognise your value and see your authenticity as solid ground for them to tread as they step forward.

When you do the rounds on podcasts, you could get pretty bored churning out the same old anecdotes. In fact, each podcast gives you a new opportunity to serve a completely unique audience. No two podcast audiences are exactly the same, so with each you have a chance to gear your story to their specific needs. The podcaster knows their listeners and has refined the format and types of guest they have on in order to serve them. Take their lead from this. What do they require from you? What are you here to teach, advise or signal specifically for them? Imagine the individual who typically represents this audience. Why are they listening? Why has the podcast host chosen you, of all the guests they could have picked? What is it about your story that serves this person? What do they need to hear right now?

Giving is receiving

Here you are giving your time, being a guide, serving others, sharing your story to benefit the listeners. For what? There is a value exchange. You give what you are able during this hour or so and, if you have managed to serve the audience effectively, they will come and find you. They will read your book. They will pay for your services. They will buy your products. They will contribute to your charity or campaign. When you make a difference to someone's life by being the voice they needed to hear at a particular point in their journey, they will become a fan and a follower, a client or customer, an advocate or champion. By giving, you cannot fail to receive.

EXAMPLE

I interviewed the actress Crystal Yu. She had come to the UK from Hong Kong to study dance at the age of eleven. She could barely speak English and was practically the only Chinese girl in the school, which had a highly competitive environment. She felt like an outsider. But when she discovered acting, she found that being an observer played to her hand. She could bring nuance to a character. As an actor, she had to take many rejections, so she learned to say yes to herself even when the world around her wanted to say no. Success came to her and she served as an example for many young Chinese girls. Acting is a haphazard affair so she supplemented it with teaching; in this way, she was able to pass on what she had learned, to encourage others where she had been discouraged. Her guidance for my audience, who wanted to know how to gain courage, was to not be afraid to go against the norm, and to become a teacher even when you are still a student of life.[25]

Learnings

When you go on air to share your story, you know to remember that the listener experience is about them, not you. You know that you are their guiding light, revealing wisdom from your own trials, errors and triumphs. You know that within your story are signals that will help others to find their way; that you are there to serve, not broadcast. In doing so, you know that in return you will gather a tribe of followers, fans, customers and clients.

ACTION STEPS

- Draw a stick person on piece of paper and write 'Listener' above them.
- Draw another stick person labelled 'Me/Guide'.
- Between the two figures, draw a signpost.
- Under the drawing, write five lessons you have learned from your story.
- Write in large letters, 'How can I serve you best?' and think about the answer.

25 L Hamilton, 'Saying yes to yourself when the world around you might be saying no, with actress Crystal Yu', Brave New Girl (2021), https://podcasts.apple.com/in/podcast/saying-yes-to-yourself-when-world-around-you-might/id1462548683?i=1000506843446

Getting in the flow

When you record a podcast, you might feel apprehensive or nervous. What if you panic and freeze, lose your thread or say the wrong thing? When you practise being fully aware, you will stay authentic and on point. In this section, you will learn how to go fully with the flow so that you come across as natural, relaxed and responsive to your podcast host. This is your moment to shine.

Being aware and present

In the moment that you ask yourself if you are aware, you automatically become so. You're not lost in thought, you're not ruminating or daydreaming or going down a spiral of negativity. You are looking in at yourself, examining your nerves or desire to do well, with objectivity. Every time you feel yourself drift off with a thought like 'Am I stumbling over my words?' or 'Am I making an arse of myself?', bring yourself back to this awareness. If you feel a sense of panic or fear or anxiety, breathe and allow it to pass. Think of negative thoughts or emotions not like a magnet sticking to you, but like a snowflake floating past you.

Being aware of yourself in the moment allows you to be fully present in it. If you are a visual learner/listener and the interviewer is visible on screen to you while you record, focus on their face. If you are an aural learner/listener, keep your attention on their voice. If you are a kinetic learner/listener perhaps have a pen in your hand and doodle or fiddle with a bit of Blue-Tack. To be present in each given moment is to be fully yourself, engaged and interacting with the interviewer with your attention wholly on them. In this way, your words will flow and your subconscious will supply the content. Your nerves will melt away and instead you will feel invigorated, energised and lifted by the conversation. The listener will hear this in your voice and become fully present themselves, actively listening. In this state, they will be more likely to follow up with you afterwards.

The devil of distraction

The devil of distraction wants to pull you away down a rabbit warren of worry, or tempt you to multi-task. If you feel your mind wandering to your shopping list, catch yourself, ask if you are aware and then pull your attention back to the interviewer. Don't give your mind the opportunity to wander. Your brain cannot focus on two things at once. If you can't trust yourself not to look at your phone, leave it in another room. Not only will allowing yourself to be distracted annoy the interviewer, it will knock you out of the flow of the conversation. The listeners will hear your distraction and you risk losing their attention too. Stay on point.

Drill down and let go

Scooting along the surface of a subject is dull – for you, for the interviewer and for the listener. Dare to drill down into your experiences, your expertise, your curiosity, your courage and your fears. What can you offer to this podcast, and these listeners, that they won't have heard you say anywhere else? How can you take your journey to the next level so that you can better inspire, intrigue and serve the listener? I can say I was living in Lockerbie when a jumbo jet was blown out of the sky. I can talk about the experience of walking into town the next morning and describe the Armageddon that had befallen my small Scottish town, but what I am offering is the fact that even though a devastating event can befall you, you can still come out the other side. Be open and vulnerable if you can. Do you want to sound like you're reading from an end of year report, or do you want to transport your listeners into your world? Consider your tone and the content and go all in.

You have committed to sharing your story and you have identified your no-go zones. This space you have opened up for the listener is where the magic happens. Let go of your inhibitions and resistance and dive into the conversation. You've prepared, so allow yourself to swim in the free-flowing waters between you and the host. Trust that you have all the knowledge, expertise, experience and insights you need at your disposal and let them bubble up while you give your full attention to the host's questions. If you feel yourself getting nervous or jittery, breathe consciously and focus your awareness. When you fully let go and give yourself to the experience, you will enter a state of flow. It will feel natural and easy. Explore the topic with curiosity, interest and enthusiasm. Shine your light fully.

EXAMPLE

My guest Madeleine Black wrote a book, *Unbroken*, about being gang-raped and tortured at the age of thirteen. Before the interview, I told her that she needed only to give the details she felt able to, but she said she was happy to share whatever came up. She knew she was in control because she had come out the other side. If she had still been trying to process the experience, she would need strong boundaries around what she was prepared to reveal. This is the same for you. Know where you are in your story and where you are still too raw and vulnerable to share. This is all in your control, so follow your own rules and be open and honest in the way that feels right for you.

Listen out for how she brings you something from her experience.[26]

---

26   L Hamilton, 'Is forgiveness possible after experiencing trauma? With author and speaker Madeleine Black', Brave New Girl (2021), https://podcasts.apple.com/in/podcast/is-forgiveness-possible-after-experiencing-trauma-author/id1462548683?i=1000509589435

Learnings

Your learnings from this section will enable you to give your best during your performance on every podcast you guest on. You have learned how to be fully aware and conscious of yourself as a guest discussing a particular topic. You know how to practise being fully present with your attention focused on the host. You understand the importance of ensuring there is a minimum of disruption and distraction so you can maintain your focus. You know how to drill down into your topic rather than skirting around the edges, while respecting the boundaries you've set for yourself. And you know that by allowing yourself to let go you can fully experience the conversation in all its nuance, depth and expansion. With this knowledge, you have the best chance of having an honest, intense and authentic interaction that will give the listener an interesting experience, food for thought and hope.

ACTION STEPS

- Sit tall, breathe through your diaphragm and ask yourself 'Am I aware?' This question makes you so.
- Identify whether you are an audio, visual or kinetic listener, then make sure you have relevant props to help you stay present.
- Make sure there are no distractions. Turn off your phone. Stop any email notifications.
- Remind yourself how deep you are prepared to go with your story. Make a note of your boundaries and

remember how you might be helping the listener.

- As you breathe, drop your shoulders and as you breathe out, say 'and letting go.'

Giving thanks

How do you end a guest appearance of a podcast? How you round up your interview is important for the podcast host. If you trail away, the listener feels that. Go out with a bang. Make the host feel fully appreciated and they will recommend you to other hosts. This isn't hard to do; when you're prepared, you'll finish with a flourish and set yourself up for ongoing podcast guesting success. In this section, we'll talk through a few ways you might end a podcast and how to excel in each scenario.

Quick-fire round

Not all podcasts have a quick-fire round, but many do, or use something similar to round up the interview. This will usually relate in some way to the themes and topics of the show and is a 'fun fact' style finale. It can also be quite insightful. You'll never know how your answers land but you can make them thoughtful and true to you. You've listened to at least a few of the podcast episodes, so you know the format and can prepare for the quick-fire round or whatever their final questions tend to be. You don't have to be clever with your answers, you just have to answer enthusiastically and authentically. Even if the host changes the quick-fire questions from guest to guest, you can still be prepared by opening up your mind to this style of questioning. If you aren't prepared for any kind of quick-fire, you might get flustered and freeze. Relax and go with it.

The big wind-up question

Sometimes a host will ask the same big wind-up question at the end of each episode. They might ask you to prepare for it when they send you their rough questions outline before the show or you may have to glean this information yourself from listening to the shows. On BNG, I always ask my guests how they define courage in light of the challenges they have faced and experiences they have had. Each guest's answer is different. If they haven't thought about their answer, their words will meander until they find an answer that feels right to them. I wait, as I know it will come, but I know that there will be some editing involved to give the listeners a coherent response. Try not to give the host that headache. It will be to your advantage to have a great answer up your sleeve. The listener's ears will be wide open to what you have to say, so be ready to give them a thorough and properly thought through reply.

Your message

Sometimes, in the wrapping up of the show, the host will ask about your plan or vision for the future. It may be more subtle than a direct question, but they will likely give you an opportunity to bring your message, mission or call to action to the listeners. What do you want your new fans to walk away with? Are they going to tell their friends about the great campaign you've got in the pipeline? Are they going to order your forthcoming book?

Knowing where you want to take people when the show is over will help maintain your connection with them. It is best not to frame this as a sales pitch or plug. Instead, inspire with an idea or a way they can engage with you further. Give away something for a free: an idea, a thought of the day or something they can download from your website. Whatever trail you want to leave, the thread of connection, the hope of future engagement, weave this into the wind-up of the show. Prepare a couple of sentences on this, something clear and simple that the listener will remember after the episode.

The host's thanks

As the host winds up the interview they may sum up your journey and the themes you have discussed. They may point out how courageous you are or how generous you have been with your answers. They will likely praise your achievements and wins and they may big up your business or brand. You might feel uncomfortable being held in such high esteem and celebrated for your triumphs, but you'll have to suck it up. If you blush at compliments then smile to make up for it (if you're being filmed). If it makes you want to shrink back in embarrassment, pull back your shoulders and allow the words to flow over you like warm ocean waves. You may not feel like you deserve adulation and adoration but the host has seen fit to shower you with praise in some form or another, so don't undermine them by tempering it or trying to ameliorate your discomfort. They have chosen to wind up the interview this way and the best thing you can do is graciously accept their expressions of gratitude.

Your final bow

In return, you may be given a moment to express your own thoughts on the discussion and to give thanks to your host. Something you can prepare beforehand and which the host will greatly appreciate, is a few sentences on why you think the theme of the podcast is so illuminating. If the host has been particularly insightful and guided you in a way that has led to a revelatory conversation, then you can express gratitude for that. Be appreciative and thankful. They have given you a platform for your voice, story, insights, experience and expertise, so be sure to acknowledge that in some way. A few words will be enough but the sentiment will land well with both the host and the listener and it ties up the end of the show nicely, leaving you, the host and the audience with a good feeling.

EXAMPLE

One of my guests, Nicki Bannerman, a radio broadcaster and podcast host herself, finished our interview particularly well. Clearly, as a host, she understood the benefit of a good ending, of tying up loose ends and of expressing an appreciation of the subject matter. I could see she had prepared a few words, but it didn't feel clunky or contrived. Instead, it helped bring a different perspective on the conclusion I had expressed in my summary. It was just a few sentences but it rounded out the ending, giving the listener a little takeaway as food for thought. Unless you are good at thinking on your feet or have a way with words even on the hoof, a little preparation goes a long way. Bow out gracefully and you will be remembered for it.[27]

Learnings

In this section, you've learned about how to finish with a flourish. This could be in a quick-fire round or something similar. If so, this will be clear from the format of the show and you can prepare beforehand. The same is true if the show features an overarching wind-up question. Don't be caught in the headlights. Do your homework. Have your message or giveaway ready if the host gives you the opportunity to share it.

27 L Hamilton, 'Rewriting your story helps you adapt to life events, with broadcaster Nicki Bannerman', Brave New Girl (2021), https://podcasts.apple.com/in/podcast/rewriting-your-story-helps-you-to-adapt-to-life-events/id1462548683?i=1000508489776

Should the host finish the show by summarising how awesome you are, accept the praise graciously and, in return, give thanks to the host. They will appreciate it if you have a few words ready to express why you believe their topic or themes to be of such value. And then it's over – well done!

ACTION STEPS

- Prepare for a quick-fire round if this is part of the show format.
- Prepare for a big final question. Do your homework and know what kind of questions the host typically asks at the end the show.
- Make sure you have your message or giveaway ready if you are given the opportunity to share.
- Get comfortable with the idea that you are worthy of any praise heaped on you.
- Prepare a few words of thanks for the host and appreciation of the show's theme.

Summary

By preparing for your performance you know that you will get the most out of every opportunity you get to spread your message and speak about your mission on podcasts. In this chapter, we talked about various aspects of your performance to consider when you're preparing to be a guest on multiple podcasts.

Recording preparation

Now you know about the importance of preparedness in ensuring you perform at your best. You've done all of your tech prep and have prepared a checklist of everything that needs checking before each podcast recording session.

Voice preparation

You know how to loosen your larynx and get yourself energised and focused ahead of a recording. You can be sure there will be no distractions and that you can keep your awareness on yourself and the host in the moment. You are ready for your performance.

Guiding light

You know you are on the podcast to serve, not broadcast, and that in doing so you will gather a tribe of followers, fans, customers and clients who will continue to engage with you beyond the end of the episode.

In the flow

You can be fully engaged with yourself and the host and keep the show's listeners at the front of your mind. By being actively aware in the moment you can allow your answers to flow from your authentic self and the conversation will feel easy.

Give thanks

You know how you want to wind up and what you are thankful for. You know you deserve any praise that is given to you and you can accept the host's gratitude for your contribution with graciousness, and give thanks in return.

SIX

Spread Your Wings

There is a lot of mileage to be had out of your podcast appearances. The podcast host will of course do their share of the work in promoting the episode, but in doing so their aim is to build the podcast brand as a whole. From your perspective, your feature is another way to build your tribe and communicate different aspects of your story, message and mission. The episode will be evergreen in that, over time, people will continue to find and listen to it, but when it airs is the best opportunity to bring it to the world's attention. If you are appearing on lots of podcasts then you need to show that each episode benefits listeners in a unique way. What particular aspect can you highlight when spreading the word about the different podcasts you appear on? Remember the job is not done when you switch off your mic. Now it's time to flex your marketing muscle.

Upon finishing this final chapter, you will know how to maximise your appearance on each podcast. In it, we will cover four steps or stages to promote the episode post-recording:

• Shout out

• Engaging on socials

- Episode airs

- Conclusion

Being an active sharer of podcast content is not just something to do as a gesture of appreciation to the podcast host for having you on the show, it is a vital part of your marketing strategy. Don't waste this opportunity to spread your wings and gather a greater flock in your wake.

Shout out

You think you've done the work, but you need to leave your trail. Make this about the message and it can be fun. In the shout out stage, you follow through, build an ongoing relationship with the podcast host and their fans and followers. This starts the moment you finish recording; you want to start the rallying cry for people to listen to your episode long before it airs.

You get such a buzz from doing an interview, sharing your story, digging deep into the things that matter, drilling down into the pain points and lessons learned and celebrating your successes, you're straight away in a great place to start blowing the trumpet for the podcast interview. You're on a high in the immediate afterglow so this is a good time to talk across your social channels about your experience of being interviewed. This gets your current audience to sit up, get excited and subscribe to the podcast so they'll know when your episode goes live. If you tag the podcast host they may join in the conversation and mutual respect exchange; if they do, their followers will have a chance to get to know who you are and follow you even before they have heard your episode. Embrace the warm fuzzy feeling of making a new virtual friend and sharing the love.

Make sure your message is clear so that the podcast host can impart that in their show notes. Sometimes they give you a spot at the end to share where listeners can find you or what freebie you have to offer and where it can be downloaded. This moment in the process in important because, as much as it's lovely that the audience has enjoyed your story, you do want them to connect with you beyond the podcast. There have been many times that I have taken note of a guest's book and bought it there and then, or gone and immediately watched a documentary they have been in, or downloaded a free guide.

Remember the podcast's DNA

When shouting about your episode, remind yourself of the podcast's DNA and make sure that you align your values with theirs in all your promotion. If their DNA is courage, use your examples of finding courage. If it is about good relationships, talk about your experience of a good relationship and how it came about. Think about the podcast listeners who you want to join your gang. They like that particular podcast for its DNA so when you show that your experiences and values are aligned with it, they will be curious about you and want to find out more.

Subscribe, download, rate and review

Even before your episode comes out you can start preparing the groundwork for it being a hit. Hopefully, you have already subscribed to the podcast, but if you haven't, do it now. It shows respect and gratitude to the podcast host but also benefits you. If you subscribe, give it five stars and leave a great review; then you are helping to boost the algorithms, which means that more people can find the show and help push it up the charts.

The same goes for downloading. You don't have to download every episode of the podcast but the more you do, the more you help boost the show. My favourite phrase is, 'We all rise by lifting each other' – this is never truer than in the podcasting world. When you download other people's episodes you are again encouraging the algorithms to put that podcast in front of more people, helping to increase its visibility among the millions of other podcasts. All this means that when your episode airs, the show overall will have already gained more traction, which is great for you. It means more people listening to the podcast, which means more people to hear you tell your story, engage with you, trust you and follow you.

EXAMPLE

I had Tava O'Halloran as a guest on BNG. She is the author of *Queen of Clubs*, a white-knuckled memoir of a girl versus the universe.

Tara knew that by appearing on podcasts she was helping to promote her book, so in the lead-up to her episode being aired she flagged up the show and did a few teasers. She also subscribed and downloaded lots of episodes and got everyone she knew to do the same. The podcast downloads soared, ready for her grand entrance on the week her episode aired.[28]

Learnings

Your first opportunity to publicise your podcast episode, and so yourself, is immediately after the interview when you're still basking in the warm glow of the conversation, so do a mini announcement or teaser straightaway. You know to make sure at this point that the host has got the correct, up-to-date information about your website and any freebies you're offering the listeners, and remind yourself of the podcast's DNA so that you align yourself to the show's listeners in your promotions. You know the importance of subscribing, rating and reviewing the show and downloading as

---

28 L Hamilton, 'When your house of cards comes crashing down, with Queen of Clubs author Tava O'Halloran', Brave New Girl (2021), https://podcasts.apple.com/in/podcast/when-your-house-cards-comes-crashing-down-queen-clubs/id1462548683?i=1000517137700

many episodes as possible to push it up the rankings and attract more listeners. By helping promote the show you are also helping to promote yourself.

ACTION STEPS

- Announce the interview immediately after recording.
- Make sure your message is clear and the host has up to date contact information for you and knows where listeners can get your freebies.
- Align yourself with the podcast's DNA in your promotions to connect with listeners.
- Subscribe, rate and review the show.
- Download lots of episodes.

Engage on socials

Once you've done the podcast, announced it and promoted your episode when it comes out, you might think that's job done. But remember why you did it in the first place: it wasn't just for fun, it is part and parcel of your marketing and PR strategy. You are trying to build your reputation, to promote your product, campaign or service and to build your clan. It would be a shame to stop at the point when you can be most effective at building engagement. Many podcast guests leave it for the podcaster to do all the work in continuing to promote the episode after it's released, but this is a wasted opportunity. It's hard work keeping on top of all the socials but now you have some good material to share, use it.

It's not all about you

I know the fear. You don't want to brag about your show appearances, you don't want to big yourself up, you don't want to make your socials a flood of me, me, me. But that's the great thing about being a podcast guest, it's not all about you – you can make it all about celebrating the podcast and the host.

You can talk about why it is such a great podcast to listen to, what it's about, why it inspires, what themes it covers, what values it upholds, who it helps and why your people will love it. Serve your tribe by telling them all about this new discovery of yours. Then you can add that oh, by the way, you were interviewed and the host is awesome in such and such a way and your followers will love them because of this and this. Encourage your followers to download and listen to particular previous episodes that you think will resonate with them and to subscribe so that they will be sure to catch yours.

Watering holes

Much as it is important to have your established gang boost the podcast in readiness for your episode going live, the real point is to gain new followers and fans and bring them into your fold. Find out which social media platforms your podcast host mostly hangs out on and start engaging with them and their mates. Are they mainly on Facebook, Twitter, LinkedIn, Instagram, Clubhouse, TikTok, Pinterest? Where are they most active? Head over to their watering holes and start hanging out with them. Comment on and engage with their posts, stories and lives. Follow their followers and engage with them too. Get to know them, cheer them on, support them and show up for them. This is all about relationship building. It takes time, energy and commitment but unless you want tumbleweed and the sound of crickets after your episode airs and no further traction, you need to do this work. You need to go out there and make friends. This is all about creating allies and finding partners and collaborators.

Once you've found where your new tribe is hanging out, what do you post about? You can give little teasers from the show, juicy nuggets that people can relate to, or pick up on discussions being had and add your insight to the mix. On your own feed, you can post teasers and whet your gang's appetite, then in your podcast host's space you can engage with and comment on posts and share what you gained from doing the interview. Take the host's lead on this. They might want to hold some things back if the show hasn't dropped yet.

Clubhouse

Clubhouse warrants its own paragraph. As the new kid on the social media block (as of 2021) it hit the ground running, boosting the role of the audio to stellar status. Those people who have committed time to it have found their networks growing exponentially. Initially, podcasters feared the demise of the podcast – this is a platform where conversations can be had, and interviews and broadcasts can be shared with a live interactive audience. In reality, it has broadened the reach for podcasters willing to engage on Clubhouse. They can follow up on discussions had with their podcast guests, they can answer questions and interact with a larger audience and they can widen the table for people to join in and become part of their movement. Rather than shrinking the podcast market, it has elevated it. Podcasters and potential guests are meeting, connecting and partnering up. As a guest, you can use it to amplify your message. Find your podcast host on Clubhouse and meet and follow their fans; you could even run a room together on the back of your episode to discuss themes and topics raised with the audience.

Clubhouse has set the stage for a whole new world of social audio; and now there are an increasing number of apps in the space. Go have global conversations and build out from your podcast guesting experiences.

EXAMPLE

One of my guests was broadcast journalist and author Dr Mandeep Rai, who took us on a journey to 101 countries around the world, highlighting a single unique value that had defined each nation's history, culture and global influence. In her book *The Values Compass* she shows how we can apply values to better our lives and make decisions more effectively.

I interviewed her a week into Clubhouse hitting the UK. When her episode aired, she started a room to talk about her new book and I joined her to talk about some of the things we discussed on the podcast.[29]

Learnings

It is important and comforting to remember that it's not all about you. In this section, you've learned that if shameless self-promotion makes you uncomfortable, you can make it about the podcast, their listeners and your current tribe. What came up in your episode that is helpful for them? You know to find where your podcast host and their followers hang out and focus your engagement with them there. You know that at this stage it's about building relationships so that, over time, you will bring new people under your wing. In the meantime, you will be laying the groundwork for your episode going live. Use social media to drop teasers and juicy nuggets so that people are intrigued

---

29 L Hamilton, 'Learning to live by what matters most to you, with author Mandeep Rai', Brave New Girl (2021), https://podcasts. apple.com/in/podcast/learning-to-live-by-what-matters-most-to-you-author/id1462548683?i=1000505968592

and want to know more. Sow the seeds for nurturing these connections. Use all the relevant social communities and, if you haven't already, find your host on Clubhouse and start building friendships.

ACTION STEPS

- Start making noise ahead of the podcast episode going live.
- Make it about the episode, the host, their listeners and what your followers might find inspiring.
- Find your host in their social watering holes and start engaging and building a relationship with them and their followers.
- Drop teasers and juicy nuggets in anticipation of the show's release.
- If you haven't already, join Clubhouse or any social audio platform that suits your needs.

Episode airs

Yikes, you're out there. Yay, you're out there! Your podcast host lets you know that your episode is now live. This is the time to celebrate, not to be modest. By bigging up the episode when it's released you are honouring the podcaster's valiant efforts to promote you, so do them a favour and do your part to get that episode out there!

Listen

First up, listen to your show. I know for some that may feel painful, but if the show is good you should be pleasantly surprise at how well you come across. It's important to listen so that you can sing the show's praises from your own perspective. If it turned out better than you expected then that gives you a good angle: 'Wow, I was so nervous, but it turned out so well, X really brought out the best in me.' This will be more engaging to your audience than, 'Oh yeah, another show I appeared on which I totally rocked.' I'm sure you'd never say that, but you get my gist. There will be surprises in the episode and things that the host drew out of you that you can talk about and share. Listen and be inspired by the conversation, pick out titbits you can tease with.

Get the assets

The show host should send you their assets for your episode, which will use your photo with their graphics, maybe a video or sound clip, perhaps a drawing or visual quote. If they don't automatically send these assets, ask for them and say you're keen to promote the show. Visual or audio assets will help you to share in different ways and on various platforms. As a host myself, I always do a drawing/cartoon of the guest, in which I try to sum up who they are and their message. Guests love this because it gives them something to share and talk about while focusing less on them and more about the picture and the episode. Hosts generally won't be producing original artworks for you, but they will usually create a graphic with your photo and their podcast imagery. This is a nice visual to share. If the host doesn't give you anything (which is rare), why not create your own? Even if creativity is not your bag, there are apps like Canva that you can use to make a sleek, professional visual – ask the host for any logos they would like you to use.

Get the blurb

Writing up the blurb for the show is an art. The host has to condense the episode into a short paragraph, highlighting the best bits while still including a bit of a tease. Ask for this summary or lift it from the show notes. It will save you time and a headache trying to write something yourself. Leave it to the host and then borrow their blurb – they won't mind, they have written it to be read, so the more it is shared the better. You can add something personal at the beginning, followed by their paragraph. If you do this, it's always good to start with a question relating to the themes and topics raised in the episode. This immediately engages the audience; they can't help but think about their answer – and then you've hooked them. If the title that the host created is a good one, use that too. Make the most of anything that will catch the attention of potential listeners and draw them to your show.

Share, share, share

Once you have your visual assets, blurb and catchy intro or intriguing question, you're ready to take to the socials. Have a social media campaign in place for the week the episode airs, this is the major chance to catch people's attention and encourage them to listen. Start by reposting whatever the host puts up, but do your own thing too. You know your audience so you can set your tone for them, which might be slightly different depending on the platform. Try and spread the message across all your channels, including your email list, on different days across the whole week. It is easy to think that you are bombarding people but the truth is that very little gets through the noise of their feed, so you need to keep on sharing. Find different ways to do this to keep it interesting, such as humour if the subject matter allows, or getting personal on a delicate or intimate subject – each of these approaches engage people on different levels.

Review

And now head back to the podcast platform and leave a review. It might sound strange to leave a review for your own episode, but no one but you has had the experience of being interviewed about your story, the particular topics you discussed as they relate to the podcast theme, your engagement with the host, and your feelings on listening to how the show played out. See this as another way to broadcast your message through authentic appreciation for the experience, the support of the host and the opportunity they gave you. Leaving a trail in those first seven days, wherever you can, will help boost the downloads and bring listeners into your world.

EXAMPLE

A recent guest on BNG was a terrific promoter, and it showed in the downloads. One day in and it was the most first day downloads that we'd ever had. She texted me and said she had been overwhelmed with messages from old friends, colleagues and customers who had been inspired by her journey. The title of the episode was 'Your "bear" necessities of life with jewellery designer Lisa Harris', and the subtitle was 'What is your talisman? The one that gives you courage in times of doubt and fear. For Amulette founder Lisa Harris, her lucky mascot is a bear; a symbol of bravery, strength and protection.' Lisa fully committed to using the experience and the exposure to engage with her people in a different way. She opened up to them with her story and they responded in kind. Listeners engaged with her on many levels, depending on how her words affected them. The responses were personal and appreciative because she had shared a deeper meaning to her brand.[30]

---

30 L Hamilton, 'Your "bear" necessities of life with jewellery designer designer Lisa Harris', Brave New Girl (2021), https://podcasts. apple.com/in/podcast/your-bear-necessities-life-jewellery-designer-lisa/id1462548683?i=1000517947059

Learnings

You know that listening to your podcast episode will help you to share your experience of the show in an authentic way. You know to ask the host for any visual and sound assets along with the episode blurb so that you can repurpose these to help promote the show among your social community. You also know that you can create your own assets, such as teasers and questions, highlighting the themes and topics that cropped up. Talk about how it made you feel and what surprising elements came up for you. Engage with the host via their socials and rev up the exposure on yours. Post across all your channels and talk about it with whomever you can, whenever you can. This is time to celebrate – and expect messages of appreciation and support.

- Listen to the episode.
- Get visual and sound assets from the host.
- Get the blurb from the host and add to it with your own teaser or question.
- Post and engage about the episode across all your social channels.
- Leave a review of the episode.

Conclusion

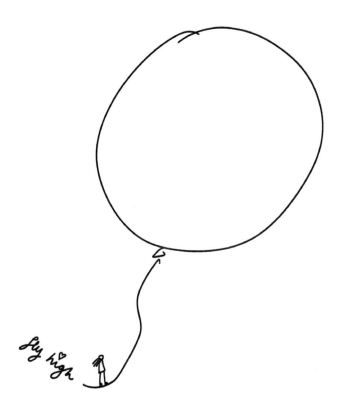

Once you have been through the whole process of guesting on a podcast a few times, you'll start to get a feel for it. Like any craft, practice makes perfect. Over time, you'll get a sense of the right kinds of podcasts for you. But consistency is key, just as it is in other areas of your marketing. A few social posts bashed out every so often isn't going to get you far, and the same is true for podcast guesting. It has a snowball effect. The more shows you guest on, the more you'll be invited onto. This requires a steady flow of pitches from you, ideally on a weekly basis. You will collect plenty of 'no's' on the way and, much as it would be fantastic to leap straight onto the big shows, the likelihood is that you'll swim with the minnows first and build up to the bigger names with a wider reach. This is a long game.

As with any game, you should have fun with it. You're getting the chance to talk about your favourite subject, the thing you're most interested in, your passion. You are bringing visibility to your expertise. You are finding your people and growing your tribe. You are having intimate conversations full of intention and that can have a positive impact. Your words are flying into the ears of people ready to hear them. You never know who you might affect, inspire and encourage. Give your best to the airwaves and leave a trail for listeners to follow.

Podcasting gives power to your voice. We all rise by sharing our stories and we are all lifted by listening to and learning from those of others. Choose courage and dare to share.

Acknowledgements

Thank you to my partner, Pablo, for his never-ending support and cheerleading. To my children, Sol and Ruby, who helped me set up Silk Studios and who inspire me with their courage and vision and remind me to stay youthful in my thinking and imagineering. To my parents, who have always supported me. To my friends, who cheerlead, celebrate and commiserate with me. To my team, who help me work on the business and not in it. To Rethink Press, for believing in this book and helping me to give birth to it. To my Brave New Girl podcast guests, who bring their courageous stories to the mic. To my Silk clients, who dare to share their experiences and expertise globally across the airwaves. To my own scribbly story, which continues to keep me on my toes. And to my character, Brave New Girl, who appeared from nowhere and has made all the difference.

Contributors

The following people have given their kind permission to have their interviews or materials used in examples in the book.

Tina Bernstein, designer and founder of Mapology Guides

Emma Campbell, author, speaker, columnist and long-term cancer thriver

Sharon Walters, artist and educator, @london_artist1

Nik Southern, founder of Grace and Thorn

Elizabeth Frood, Egyptologist

Sarah Hickson, professional photographer

Ali Criado-Perez, registered nurse/MSF medical team leader

Uju Asika, blogger, creative consultant and author of *Bringing up Race*

Tamsyn Wood, health and wellness blogger

Karen Arthur, fashion creative and founder of the Menopause While Black podcast

Hannah Turner, founder of ceramics company Hannah Turner Ltd

Astrid and Miyu jewellers' podcast 'After Hours'

Emily Syphas, founder of Sober and Social

Vix Munro, founder of Money Badassary

Dawn Mcgruer, founder of Business Consort – Digital and Social Media Academy, and host of Dawn of a New Era podcast

Megan Accardo, business coach (www.meganaccardo.com) for the pitch letter template

Pam Millington, farmer

Annabelle Mu'azu, creative entrepreneur and founder/visionary (www.Ihuoma.co)

Dr Vidhi Patel, holistic medical consultant, Ayurveda and homeopathy expert and consulting nutritionist

Penny Power OBE, founder of Business is
Personal

Crystal Yu, actor, filmmaker, educator

Madeleine Black, author and podcast host of
Unbroken

Nicki Bannerman, radio and podcast host

Tava O'Halloran, author and creative director

Dr Mandeep Rai, author and journalist

Lisa Harris, jewellery designer and founder of
Amulette, London

The Author

Lou Hamilton is an artist, author, award-winning film-maker, host of the Brave New Girl podcast and founder of Silk Studios, the podcast guest agency. Whatever the medium, she has made it her mission to use creativity to make a positive impact in the world, through sharing stories of people who have overcome fears, challenges and adversity, with documentaries that draw on social issues and in her books, *Brave New Girl: How to Be Fearless* and *FEAR LESS*. She believes everyone has a story to tell and that by giving voice to their experiences, sharing their challenges and lessons learned, they can help inspire and encourage others to live their best lives. This is why she hosts her podcast, it's why she helps people to guest on other podcasts and it's why she wrote and illustrated this book.

⊕ www.silk-studios.co.uk

Lightning Source UK Ltd.
Milton Keynes UK
UKHW021418180921
390797UK00009B/218